55
Crochet Gifts
For the Home

Angela King

David & Charles

ABBREVIATIONS

	UK	USA		UK	USA
approx	approximately		no	number	
beg	beginning		opp	opposite	
CC	contrasting colour		patt	pattern	
ch	chain		PC	popcorn	
cm	centimetres(s)		prev	previous	
col	colour		quad tr	quadruple treble	triple treble
cont	continue		quin tr	quintuple treble	quadruple treble
dc	double crochet	single crochet	R	right	
dec	decrease		rem	remaining	
dia	diameter		rep	repeat	
DK	double knitting	knitting worsted	RH	right hand	
dtr	double treble	treble	rhs	right-hand side	
foll	following		rnd	round	
4 ply	four ply	sport	RS	right side	
g	gramme(s)		sext tr	sextuple treble	quintuple treble
grp	group		sp(s)	spaces(s)	
htr	half treble	half double crochet	sq(s)	square(s)	
in	inch(es)		ss	slip stitch	
inc	increase		st(s)	stitch(es)	
L	left		tog	together	
LH	left hand		tr	treble	double crochet
lhs	left-hand side		ttr	triple treble	double treble
m	metre(s)		WS	wrong side	
MC	main colour		yrh	yarn round hook	yarn over
mm	millimetre(s)				

Pine furniture, china and glass, featured in the photographs,
by courtesy of Country Pine & Collectibles,
Sidmouth Street, Devizes, Wilts

A DAVID & CHARLES BOOK

Copyright © Text and line illustrations Angela King 1993
Photographs by Di Lewis
First published 1993

Angela King has asserted her right to be identified as author of this work in accordance with the Copyright, Designs and Patents Act 1988.

A catalogue record for this book is available from the British Library.

ISBN 0 7153 9957 8

Typeset in Goudy Old Style by
ABM Typographics Ltd, Hull, England
and printed in Italy
by New Interlitho SpA
for David & Charles
Brunel House Newton Abbot Devon

Contents

INTRODUCTION · 4

NOTES · 6   TECHNIQUES · 7
FILET CROCHET · 11   SEWING AND TRIMMING · 15
BLOCKING AND PRESSING · 15

CHAPTER ONE – THE HALL · 17
Filet Door Curtain · Table Runner · Purse · Flowerpot Cover · Shawl · Bag · Ladies' Gloves

CHAPTER TWO – THE LIVING ROOM · 29
Key Bookmark · Lampshade · Playing Cards Envelope · Sofa Throwover · Antimacassar
Picture Frame · Small Blanket · 'Windows' Cushion · Needlecase · Table Centre · Place Mat

CHAPTER THREE – THE KITCHEN · 45
Ice Cream Border · Coffee Jar Cover · Egg Cosy · Simple Rug · Filet Jam Pot Cover ·
Filet Shelf Edging · Jug Cover · Basin Holders · Plant Hanging

CHAPTER FOUR – TEATIME · 57
Lacy Doily · Traycloth · Tablecloth · Cake Frill · Tea Cosy · Napkin Rings

CHAPTER FIVE – THE BEDROOM · 69
Bedspread · Hot Water Bottle Cover · Filet Bedlinen Edgings · Duchesse Set ·
Table Top or Chest Cover · Small Cushion

CHAPTER SIX – THE BATHROOM · 81
Toilet Roll Cover · Bathmat · Filet Guest Towel Edging · Small Curtain ·
Lavender Bags · Tissue Box Cover

CHAPTER SEVEN – THE NURSERY · 89
Filet Valance · Canopy and Frill · Dress · Matinée Coat · Bonnet · Baby Shawl

CHAPTER EIGHT – CELEBRATION · 101
Ribbon · Bell · Christmas Ball · Christmas Tree Decorations · Christmas Fairy · Snowman ·
Basket · Floral Card · Penny-Farthing Card

EDGINGS, BRAIDS AND INSERTIONS · 117

YARN MANUFACTURERS · 127   INDEX · 128

Introduction

Of all the traditional crafts, crochet must be one of the most
versatile. It can be made into a wide range of beautiful items,
including objects for the home, clothing, jewellery, flowers, toys,
containers and trimmings for all types of needlework – I've even
seen a crocheted hammock and chess set!
Crochet is quick to do and can be applied both prettily and
practically, and as well as the huge assortment of commercial yarns
available, wire, string, cord, ribbon or even dyed tights cut spiral-
fashion into two continuous lengths can be used.

Bearing in mind the usefulness and versatility of crochet, this book is arranged in chapters which invite the reader to take an imaginary tour through a house, stepping first into the hall, then the sitting room and so on room by room, where a variety of gifts are carefully laid out. In the hall you will find a pair of gloves and a door curtain; in the bedroom a pillowcase edging and pretty mats for a dressing

table; you can pause to enjoy tea time, and then discover a lacy crocheted shawl for a new baby in the nursery. In some rooms you may care to stop and linger awhile, and be inspired to make one of the gifts displayed there.

Throughout the book, the patterns have been graded according to difficulty – so whether you've enjoyed crochet for years or are just getting started, there will be a project to suit your ability. To help you decide which of the many designs to tackle, look for * which indicates 'easy', ** some 'experience' necessary, or *** a 'challenge'.

There is variety in the scale of projects, too, which range from a sofa throwover made with traditional Granny squares down to little decorations for a Christmas tree. Some of the

designs are nostalgic, like the antimacassar, some more modern, such as the bathmat. There are also 'light' or 'heavy' styles – for example, the lacy cotton doily and the kitchen valance. Trimmings – edgings, braids and insertions – are also included towards the end of the book. Hooks used range from 1.25–8.00mm, and each pattern gives measurements in both imperial and metric, while abbreviations and their equivalents for American readers are explained.

While designing the projects for this book, it occurred to me that whilst most women can sew and knit, far fewer can crochet. Many wish they had the ability but either have not found the time to learn, are deterred by their belief that it is difficult, or have become discouraged soon after starting and have given up. With this in mind, I have included a Techniques section especially for the be-

ginner, in which I've tried to ensure that both text and diagrams are absolutely clear and simple to follow. The stitch count given for each of the basic stitches will further facilitate learning. Also included are basic filet crochet instructions, where a knowledge of the crocheted chain and treble stitch is all that's required. Here, I've tried to explain not only the method of working filet,

Notes

1 Tension is the number of sts and rows to equal a given measurement: in this book it is mostly calculated over 10cm (4in), and has been specified for all patterns where essential or important to the completed size of an article. It has also been given as a gauge, especially useful when a particular yarn is discontinued or unobtainable. Alter hook size, if necessary, to obtain correct tension.

When a stated yarn is unavailable for any reason, an alternative can be used provided it is equally suited to the particular article and works to the given tension. The total amount required, however, may differ.

2 Purchase a good quality **yarn**. Yarn plys often vary considerably from one manufacturer to another: for example, one DK yarn can be of a similar thickness to another in 4-ply. Cheap yarns can soon lose their bulk; try working and undoing a few rows once or twice and immediately reworking them!

If possible, purchase all the yarn required for an article in one go, and check on the labels that the dye number is the same throughout. Even a white shade can vary between lots, and any difference can be just as noticeable as with a coloured yarn.

3 Use only the best quality **hooks**. These should then last for years, and will be an advantage to the learner. (See table below.)

4 Multiples. At the start of some of the patt instructions in this book, it states:

(Make x no of ch, or any no divisible by . . .). This is an indication that the article or trimming can be made to any size required, from the patt.

A length of ch divisible by 10–2 means any multiple of ten minus two, for example, 28ch (=30–2); 38ch (40–2); or 48ch (50–2), and so on. In this book it does not mean divisible by 8. Therefore, a length of ch divisible by 6+2 will be any number that can be divided by 6, with 2 added on, for example, 50ch, 62ch, and so on.

5 Basic **crochet techniques** sometimes differ to a small degree and it is important to understand two of the variations in particular:

(i) A turning ch may not always count as the 1st st of a row, but is sometimes made only to bring the hook into line for the start of a new row. With a straight piece of crochet of 10sts, all 10sts after the turning ch – from the 1st st to the 10th st – will be worked into. Therefore, at the end of a row, the previous row's turning ch will not be worked into.

(ii) On the 1st row of crochet, the positions for initial insertion of the hook are consecutive and therefore easy to remember. For example, 1dc into 2nd ch from hook (the missed ch positioning the 1st dc); 1htr into 3rd ch from hook; 1tr into 4th ch from hook, and so on (the missed chs forming a st). Instructions for initial hook placement do not always agree, but patterns will state which ch st to employ.

Whilst learning to crochet, it will be helpful always to count the sts of each row.

◆

USEFUL ITEMS

For working crochet:
Small safety pins for use as markers
Medium safety pins for holding pieces together for seaming
Small, sharp scissors
Ruler and coiled steel rule for measuring small and large areas
Large wool needle (blunt) for threading thick yarns, string, etc
Medium size polythene bag to keep yarn clean whilst in use – knot opening, leaving space for yarn end to come through

For blocking and pressing work:
Pins
Small cotton cloth
Water spray canister

Techniques

Learning to crochet is much easier at the very beginning if either a light-to-medium coloured DK handicraft cotton or any DK yarn is used, with a No 4.00, 4.50, or 5.00 crochet hook. Left-handed crocheters should reverse L and R instructions.
(N.B. In some illustrations the hook has been omitted for clarity.)

◆ CHAIN (ch)

Make a slip-knot and insert hook. Tighten loop enough for it to slide easily on the main part of the hook. Keep the knot fairly tight.

Allow the upper part of the hook to rest between thumb and first finger. Temporarily hold top of slip-loop in position with the second finger, right hand.

Wind yarn from ball round hook (yrh) with the left hand. Maintain control of the yarn by lightly gripping it between both second and

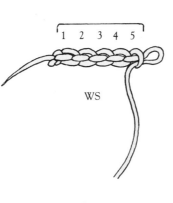

5ch

RS

WS

1 2 3 4 5

third finger, and closed fourth finger of same hand. (You may discover a more comfortable method of controlling the yarn for yourself, in time.) Hold knot with thumb and first finger, left hand, and draw the yarn through loop on hook. One chain stitch made. (1ch)

Hands should be in a relaxed position, but in control of hook and yarn. Again, temporarily hold in position top of loop on hook (not counted as a stitch), yrh, and complete another ch st.

Altogether, make 5ch.

Right side (RS) of the base chain (sometimes called foundation chain) is facing. Now turn work over to look at wrong side (WS) of chain. Note the centre, horizontal line of loops.

SLIP STITCH (ss)

Retain the 5ch made.

Slip stitch (ss) is a shallow stitch used mostly for joining or shaping. Insert hook into 2nd ch from hook, under top two strands of yarn. Yrh. With one movement, draw yarn through both the 2nd ch from hook and loop on hook. 1ss made.

The first ch st was missed; the second ch was worked into, therefore 3ch remain unworked.

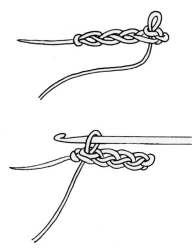

Work 1ss into each of remaining 3ch. 4ss made. (If you have any difficulty in inserting the hook, the chains may be too tight: this can easily be remedied by using a size larger hook for the chains and reverting to the original hook for foll rows.)

DOUBLE CROCHET (dc)

Make 5ch.

Row 1: Insert hook into 2nd ch from hook (always under top two strands of yarn, unless otherwise stated). Yrh, draw yarn through. There are two loops on hook.

Yrh again. Draw yarn through both the loops on hook. 1dc made.

Insert hook into next ch, yrh, draw yarn through, yrh, draw yarn through both loops on hook. 2dc made. Dc to end, by working 1dc into each of remaining 2ch. 4dc made. RS is facing.

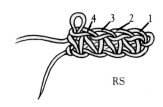

RS

In all, 4sts have been worked. Missing the 1st ch helps to position the 1st dc. The hook could also initially be inserted into the 3rd ch from hook. Here the 2 missed chs would *form* the 1st dc. In both cases, the 1st dc row has one fewer sts than the base ch. The foll rows are worked in the same way.

Row 2: Make 1ch and turn the crochet, or turn and then make the 1ch, so that WS is facing. (It is

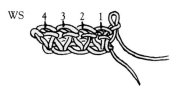

WS

rather awkward to insert hook into the 1st st on rows, so one – or more – turning ch counts as the 1st st of a new row.)

After the turning ch, insert hook into 2nd st and make 1dc. Work 2dc to end of row, turn.

Row 3: Make 1ch for 1st st, 1dc into each of next 3sts, turn.

The last st worked into will be the 1st st (turning ch) of the previous row.

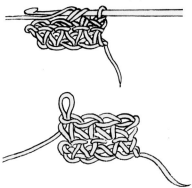

Sometimes 2ch are made for the 1st dc, and whether 1ch or 2ch are used mostly depends on tension and/or yarn being used. (Try loosening the loop on hook before making the 1ch, and notice any difference.)

Work another few rows of dc on the 4sts. Try inserting hook under only one strand (either top back or top front). You will note that this produces a slightly different effect.

FASTENING OFF

Finish your crochet by fastening off. To do this, break the yarn (leaving enough of the yarn for darning in), and draw the end through the loop on the hook.

HALF TREBLE (htr)

Make 5ch.

A half treble is taller than a dc, so the hook is inserted into the 3rd ch from hook, and at the end of rows you will have to make 2ch to turn.

Row 1: Yrh, insert hook into 3rd ch from hook. Yrh, draw yarn through, yrh, draw yarn through all 3 loops on hook. The 2 missed ch sts have formed the 1st htr, so 2htr have been made.

Yrh, insert hook into next ch, yrh, draw yarn through, yrh, draw yarn through all 3 loops on hook. Work 1htr into next st (last ch). 4htr.
The 1st htr row has one fewer sts than the base ch.

Row 2: Make 2ch for 1st htr. (Inserting hook under the two strands on top of the st), work 1htr into each of next 3sts. The last of these sts is worked into 2nd ch of the 2ch of the previous row.
Rep Row 2 twice more. Break yarn and fasten off.

◆

TREBLE (tr) DC

Make 5ch.
A treble is the tallest of the 3 basic sts, so the hook is inserted into the 4th ch from hook, and 3ch made to turn. Note that there are 3 'stages' in making a tr.

Row 1: Yrh, insert hook into 4th ch from hook, yrh, draw yarn through, yrh, draw yarn through 2 of the 3 loops on hook, yrh, draw yarn through the 2 remaining loops on hook. The 3 missed ch sts have formed the 1st tr, so 2tr have been made.
Work 1tr into last st.
The 1st tr row has two fewer sts than the base ch.
Turn, and make 3ch for the 1st tr.
Row 2: 1tr into next st (hook under top two strands at left of centre).

Work 1tr into top of last st. This last st was formed from the ch sts missed on Row 1. Turn.
Work two more rows in tr st. Break yarn and fasten off.

◆

DOUBLE TREBLE (dtr)

Make 5ch.

Row 1: Yrh twice. Insert hook into 5th ch from hook, yrh, draw yarn through, yrh, draw yarn through 2 of the 4 loops on hook, yrh, draw yarn through 2 of the 3 loops on hook, yrh, draw yarn through 2 loops on hook. 2dtr made. Turn.

Row 2: 4ch for 1st dtr. Yrh twice, complete 1dtr into next st (top of 4 missed base ch). 2dtr made.
Break yarn and fasten off.

◆

TRIPLE TREBLE (ttr)

Make 14ch.
Row 1: Yrh 3 times, insert hook into 6th ch from hook, yrh, draw yarn through, yrh, draw yarn through 2 of the 5 loops on hook, yrh, draw yarn through 2 of the 4 loops on hook, yrh, draw yarn through 2 of the 3

loops on hook, yrh, draw yarn through the 2 rem loops on hook.
Ttr to end (10sts).
Taller trebles can be made similarly, simply by altering the no of times the yarn is wound around hook, and drawing yarn through 2 loops at a time as before. The following table gives the no of times the yarn is wound around hook. Try working a row of each type of treble.

tr	1
dtr	2
ttr	3
quad tr	4
quin tr	5
sext tr	6, etc

◆

TURNING CHAINS

Usual no of ch made for the 1st st of a row.

ss	1 (or work the 1st ss into 1st st of row)
dc	1 (or 2, often dependent on yarn thickness)
htr	2 HDC
tr	3 DC
dtr	4 TREBLE
ttr	5
quad tr	6
quin tr	7
sext tr	8, etc

See Note 5, p6

◆

DOUBLE CHAIN

This can be used as an attractive cord or as an alternative base ch.
Make 2ch. Work 1dc into 2nd ch from hook, inserting hook under top strand only. *Work 1dc into last dc

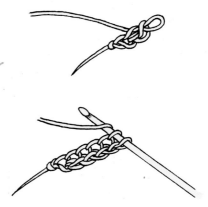

made, inserting hook under single strand at left of dc.

Rep from * to required length. Break yarn and fasten off.

◆

INCREASING

This is simply achieved by working 2 or 3 sts into one st of previous row. To increase at row ends, work the increase into the 2nd st from each end.

9sts
7sts

This helps maintain neat edges to the crochet. Temporarily a coloured thread can be used to mark increases so that they are more easily seen.

To increase more than 2sts at the beg of a row, make a ch for each st required, plus 1ch for dc or htr, 2ch for tr, and so on. For an increase of 5ttr, therefore, make 9ch.

Start the next row as you would after a base ch, and work 1dc into 2nd ch from hook, or 1dtr into 5th ch from hook, etc.

To increase more than 2sts at the end of a row, extend the relevant row by joining on a separate piece of yarn, with a ss, make a number of ch sts to equal the number of sts required.

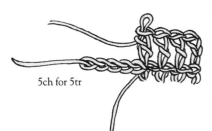

5ch for 5tr

quired and draw yarn end loosely through last ch st to secure. (Or make one extra ch st, draw end through and pull to tighten.)

◆

DECREASING

A decrease can sometimes be made by simply missing a st, although this may leave a noticeable hole. A better method is to work 2sts (or more) together.

dc2tog: Insert hook into next st, yrh, draw yarn through, insert hook into foll st, yrh, draw yarn through, yrh, draw yarn through all 3 loops on hook.

dc3tog: As dc2tog but work over next 3sts, instead of 2sts, and draw yarn through all 4 loops on hook.

htr2tog: Yrh, insert hook into next st, yrh, draw yarn through, yrh, insert hook into foll st, draw yarn through, yrh, draw yarn through all 5 loops on hook.

htr3tog: As htr2tog but work over next 3sts, instead of 2sts, and draw yarn through all 7 loops on hook.

tr2tog: Yrh, insert hook into next st, yrh, draw yarn through, yrh, draw yarn through 2 of the loops on hook, yrh, insert hook into foll st, yrh, draw yarn through, yrh, draw yarn through 2 of the loops on hook, yrh, draw yarn through all 3 loops on hook.

tr3/4/5/6tog: As tr2tog but work over next 3/4/5/6sts, and draw through all 4/5/6/7 loops on hook.

dtr2tog: *Yrh twice, insert hook into next st, yrh, draw yarn through, (yrh, draw yarn through 2 loops on hook) twice*.

Rep from * to *, yrh, draw yarn through all 3 loops on hook.

To decrease at ends of rows, work the decreases into sts next to ends, to maintain neat edges.

The process of working sts together is also used for creating many lacy patterns, as well as for decreasing.

◆

CIRCLES

(Example 1: dc)

Make 4ch. Join with ss into circle (inserting hook into 1st ch made, yrh, and drawing yarn through both 1st ch st and loop on hook to make ss). (4sts).

Round 1: Make 1ch to start this round. (The 1ch puts the 1st dc on the outside of the circle.) Work 8dc (twice number of ch) into circle, that is, over 4ch into centre space of circle.

Miss 1ch, ss into 1st dc. (8sts).

The foll rounds can be worked in two ways. Either make separate rounds, with 1ch for 1st dc, and close each round with ss into this st; or make continuous rounds, omitting the ch and working around in a spiral fashion.

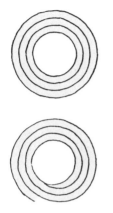

RS is facing, and the work is not turned at end of each round. (When working in a spiral, use a marker to indicate the last st of each round.)

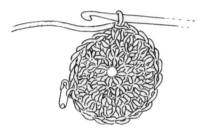

Round 2: 1ch for 1st dc, 1dc into same place as 1ch, 2dc into each foll st to end, ss into 1st dc. (8dc increased = 16sts).
Round 3: 1ch (1st dc), 2dc into next st, *1dc into next st, 2dc into next st. Rep from * to end, ss into 1st dc. (24sts).
Round 4: 1ch (1st dc), 1dc into next st, 2dc into next st, *1dc into each of next 2sts, 2dc into next st.

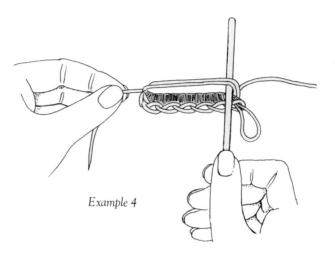

Example 4

Rep from * to end, ss into 1st dc. (32sts).
Round 5: 1ch (1st dc), 1dc into each of next 2sts, 2dc into next st, *1dc into each of next 3sts, 2dc into next st. Rep from * to end, ss into 1st dc. (40sts).
Round 6: 1ch (1st dc), 1dc into each foll st to end, ss into 1st dc. (40sts).

(Example 2: tr)
Make 4ch. Join with ss into circle.
Round 1: 3ch (1st tr), work 11tr into circle (= 3 times number of ch), ss into top (3rd) of 3ch.
Round 2: 3ch (1st tr), 1tr into same place as 3ch, 2tr into each foll st to end, ss into top of 3ch. (24sts).
Round 3: 3ch (1st tr), 2tr into next st, *1tr into next st, 2tr into next st. Rep from * to end, ss into top of 3ch. (36sts).

(Example 3: dc)
Make 2ch.
Round 1: 7dc into 2nd ch from hook.
Round 2: Work 2dc into each dc.
Round 3: *1dc into next dc, 2dc into next dc.
Rep from * to end.

(Example 4: dc)
Wind yarn twice around finger. Insert hook into space and draw yarn through to front. Make 1ch, and work dc over the 2 strands. Close circle by unhooking last loop, placing hook temporarily into circle, and pulling on the free end.

◆
CHANGING COLOUR
Work the last stage of a stitch in the next colour you wish to use, so that the loop on the hook is in the new colour.

FILET CROCHET

Filet crochet consists simply of trebles and chains (worked as blocks and spaces) to form a variety of patterns. Numerous household and fashion items can be made with filet crochet, and it is relatively easy to create personalised designs of letters, shapes, flowers and even complete pictures, by setting out a pattern similar to an ordinary crossword. The crochet is then worked following this chart. Each horizontal line represents one row. Each vertical line on a row represents one treble st. Each space between these vertical lines can be filled in with two more trebles (for a block) or two chains (for a space).

The first row of the pattern begins at the bottom right-hand corner, the second (even) row is worked from left to right, the third (odd) row from right to left, etc. To begin a row with a space, make 5 extra ch, and work 1tr into 8th ch from hook. To begin with a block, make 3 extra ch, and work 1tr into 4th ch from hook.

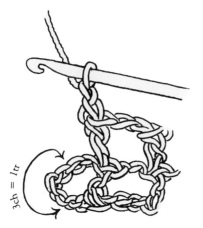

Place last tr in correct place so as to retain vertical edge to the filet crochet

Row 2: 5ch (1st tr and sp), 1tr into next tr, *2ch, miss next 2ch, 1tr into next tr.
Rep from * to end.

Filet chart 'A' (see below) begins: Make 45ch.
Row 1: 1tr into 4th ch from hook, 1tr into each of next 2ch, *2ch, miss next 2ch, 1tr into each of next 4ch. Rep from * to last 3ch, 2ch, miss next 2ch, 1tr into last ch, turn.
Row 2: 5ch (tr+2ch), *miss next 2ch, 1tr into next tr, 2ch, miss next 2tr, 1tr into next tr, 2ch. Rep from * omitting last 2ch at end of row.

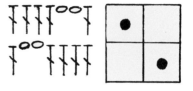

Blocks and Spaces

KEY: tr ⊺ ch ○

The 5 extra ch stand for 1tr + 2ch; the 3 extra ch for 1tr. To determine the number of ch sts to begin with, count the squares across, × 3 (1tr and 2ch for each sq) + 5 (3 for 1tr + 2ch sp), or 3 (tr block).
Therefore, the pattern for a filet background with, say, 15 spaces across × 2 spaces high, reads as follows:
Make 50ch.
Row 1: 1tr into 8th ch from hook, *2ch, miss next 2ch, 1tr into next ch. Rep from * to end, turn.

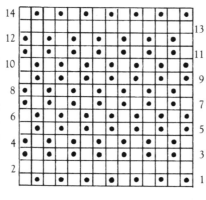

Chart A

When a block falls over a space, the 2tr are worked into the space.
The appearance of the crochet will improve if each block or space is square. This can be difficult to achieve, but it is not always essential. Try experimenting with different yarns and hook sizes, or vary the tension.
It is useful to have graph paper for making the designs; 2mm ($^1/_{10}$in) squares should enable you to see the overall picture clearly. On a very few occasions it may be advisable to elongate the design on the graph if relatively square blocks and spaces are an impossibility. A small sample of blocks and spaces using the desired yarn would need to be worked and measured first in order to correct any deficiency on graph paper. For

A rose – from sketch to a filet chart

example, a design that may be 5sqs wide and 5sqs long and in the right proportion on the paper, may need to be re-drawn as 5sqs wide and 6 or 7 sqs long.

The lacet is a stitch that can look extremely pretty when incorporated into filet crochet. It is worked with a 5ch 'bar' over two squares and two rows.

On the 1st lacet row, instead of filling two squares with the usual trs or leaving sps, make 3ch, miss 2ch or 2tr, 1dc into next tr, 3ch, miss next 2ch or 2tr, and then work 1tr as normal.

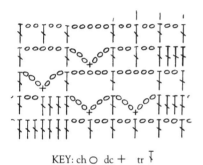

KEY: ch ○ dc + tr †

On the return row, make a bar of 5ch over the V-shaped lacet.

To work a lacet over a bar, simply

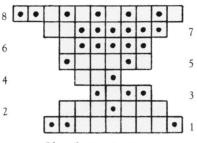

Chart for practice piece

into each of next 3tr, 5ch (= 1st tr + 2ch), miss next 2tr, 1tr into next tr, (2ch, miss next 2ch, 1tr into next tr) twice, 2tr into next sp, 1tr into next tr, (2ch, miss next 2ch, 1tr into next tr) 3 times, turn.

Row 3: Sp decs at beg and end of row: 1ss into 1st st, 1ss into each of next 2ch, 1ss into next tr, 3ch, (2tr into next sp, 1tr into next tr) twice, 2ch, miss next 2tr, 1tr into next tr, 2tr into next sp, 1tr into next tr, turn.

Row 4: Sp inc at beg and block decs at end of row: 7ch (=2ch base, 3ch for tr, 2ch top), 1tr into 1st st (last tr of prev row), 2ch, miss next 2tr, 1tr into next tr, 2tr into next sp, 1tr into

next tr, turn.

Row 5: Sp and block inc at beg; block inc at end of row: 10ch, 1tr into 8th ch from hook, 1tr into each of next 2ch, 1tr into 1st tr, 2ch, miss next 2tr, (1tr into next tr, 2ch, miss next 2ch) twice, 1tr into next ch (top of 3ch tr), do not turn. 1dtr (yarn twice round hook) into same ch as last tr made, 1dtr into base of dtr. Work 1dtr into base of dtr just made, to complete the block inc, turn.

Row 6: 5ch (1st tr + 2ch), miss 1st 3dtr, 1tr into next tr, (2tr into next sp, 1tr into next tr) 3 times, 1tr into each of next 3tr, 2tr into next sp, 1tr into last tr (5th ch), turn.

Row 7: Block inc at beg and sp inc at end of row: 5ch, 1tr into 4th ch from hook, 1tr into next tr, 1tr into 1st tr, 1tr into each of next 15tr, 2ch, miss next 2ch, 1tr into next tr, 2ch, 1ttr into same place as last tr made, turn.

Row 8: 2 block inc at beg and sp inc at end of row: 8ch, 1tr into 4th ch from hook, 1tr into each of next 4ch, 1tr into ttr.

Follow chart to end.

Techniques

◆

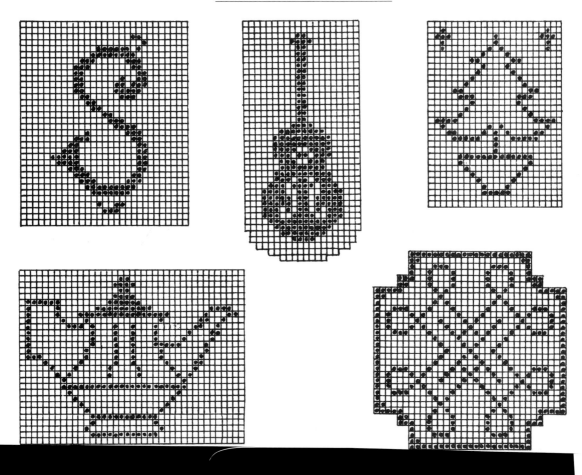

SEWING AND TRIMMING

The following sewing stitches are used for articles in the book requiring some needlework.

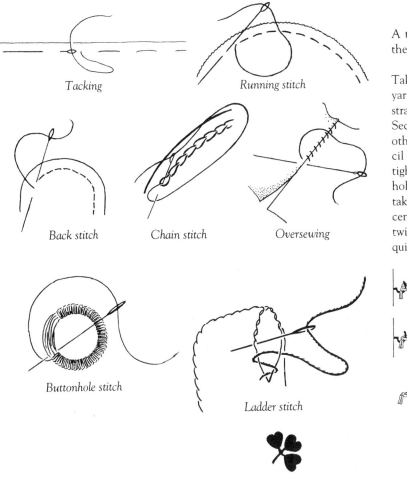

Tacking

Running stitch

Back stitch

Chain stitch

Oversewing

Buttonhole stitch

Ladder stitch

◆

TWISTED CORD

A twisted cord is used in several of the projects, and is made as follows:

Take, for example, 3 strands of DK yarn, each 1m in length. Place the strands together and knot both ends. Secure one end, insert a pencil in other end and continually spin pencil until strands are twisted together tightly but not overtwisted. Pinch hold of centre, fold cord in half, and take hold of both ends. Release centre allowing doubled cord to twist on its own, then smooth out quickly.

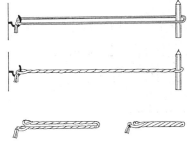

BLOCKING AND PRESSING

This is an important process to which a great deal of time and care should be given.

Blocking simply means pinning out an article to its correct shape and size prior to pressing. Pin crochet, RS down, onto a clean, padded surface, such as an ironing board or table, depending on the size of the article. Insert pins slanting slightly outwards.

For pressing, first read the direction on the label of the yarn used. This should indicate whether or not to use an iron, and if so, its heat setting and if a damp or dry cloth is required.

Very useful for blocking and pressing is a water-spray canister, which can be purchased inexpensively. Alternatively, use any thoroughly cleaned out canister which has a spray lever and screw top attachment for filling. Lightly spray

crochet, or cover with a damp cloth, and leave for a few hours to dry before removing pins. (A water spray is also invaluable when a 'damp' cloth is indicated on the yarn label, because a spray can dampen a cloth to the right degree, rather than soak it.) If pressing is absolutely necessary, use a clean iron and 'press' rather than 'iron', employing a light up and down action. Avoid the pins, which could scratch the iron's surface.

CHAPTER ONE

The Hall

Flowerpot Cover (page 21); Table Runner (page 19);
Filet Door Curtain (page 18)

FILET DOOR CURTAIN

✳

🍀 *This filet crochet curtain, with its unusual galleon design, is a pretty and practical way to lighten a dark hall or door.*

MATERIALS

6 balls white = approx 360g (13oz) or 7 balls coloured = approx 350g (12½oz) Twilleys Southern Comfort Crochet Cotton (3 ply: ball = 363/411m [400/450yd])
Hook 2.50
Spray starch for pressing (optional)

◆

TENSION

8sqs wide and 8½sqs long = 10cm (4in)sq

MEASUREMENTS

Approx 110 × 195cm (42 × 79in)

METHOD

Each space for this curtain is formed with 1dtr, 3ch, 1dtr: the 3ch space is changed to 3dtr to form a block of 5dtr. Make 7ch (dtr+3ch) for a space or 4ch (dtr) for a block at the beg of a row: at a row end, work the last dtr into 4th of 4ch or 7ch (see below). For further instructions on filet crochet, see page 11.
Start by making 344ch (85 × 4 = 340 + 4).

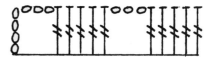

From left to right, work 7ch for 1st space. 5dtr and 3 ch form the filet blocks and spaces for the curtain

Row 1: 1dtr into 5th ch from hook, 1dtr into each foll ch to end, turn.

Row 2: 7ch (dtr + 3ch sp), (miss next 3dtr, 1dtr into each of next 5dtr, 3ch) twice, miss next 3dtr, *1dtr into next dtr, 3ch, miss next 3dtr.

Rep from * to last 17sts, (1dtr into each of next 5dtr, 3ch, miss next 3dtr) twice, 1dtr into last dtr. Cont by following the chart from 3rd row (odd rows worked from R to L).

Rep the last 2 rows of chart until curtain measures approx 195cm (79in), or required length. The final few rows can be folded back to receive a rod or wire.

TABLE RUNNER

✳ ✳

Perfect for dressing up a sideboard or festive dining table, this table runner is made all the more attractive and unusual by the shapes of the large spaces worked into it.

•

MATERIALS

50g (2oz) DMC Cebelia No 10 Crochet Cotton
Hook 1.75

•

TENSION

37dtr = 10cm (4in) across

•

MEASUREMENTS

Approx 58 × 24cm (23 × 9½in)

•

METHOD

Make 226ch (or any no. divisible by 6 + 4 for required length).

Row 1: (RS) 1dtr into 5th ch from hook, 1dtr into each foll ch to end, turn.

Row 2: 13ch (dtr + 9ch), miss 1st and next 5sts, 1dtr into next st, *9ch, miss next 5sts, 1dtr into next st. Rep from * to end, turn.

Row 3: 4ch (dtr), 3dtr into 1st dtr, *2ch – fairly loosely, 3dtr into next dtr.

Rep from * to end, working 4dtr instead of 3dtr into last dtr (4th of 13ch), turn.

Row 4: 4ch (dtr), dtr3tog (next 3sts of 1st grp). *4ch, 1dc under next 9ch and 2ch loops tog, 4ch, dtr3tog of next grp.

Rep from * to end, working dtr4tog for last grp, turn.

Row 5: 9ch (dtr + 5ch), 1dtr into top of 2nd dtr grp (slightly left of centre), *5ch, 1dtr into top of next dtr grp.

Rep from * to end, turn.

Rows 6–9: Rep rows 2–5 once more.

Row 10: 9ch (dtr + 5ch), 1dtr into 2nd dtr, *5ch, 1dtr into next dtr.

Rep from * to end, turn.

Rep last row 5 times more, and Rows 2–5 twice more. Break yarn and fasten off. Rejoin to 4th of 9ch at beg of last row.

Final row: 4ch (dtr), *1dtr into each of next 5ch, 1dtr into next dtr.

Rep from * to end.

•

EDGING

Do not turn – work along side. Note that there are 14 sps and 4 'acorns' along side (see below).

Work 7dtr into 1st sp, 1dc into centre (side) of 1st acorn, 5dtr into next sp, 3dtr into st before next sp, 5dtr into 3rd sp, 1dc into next acorn centre, 6dtr into 4th sp, (1dtr into st before next sp, 3dtr into next sp) 6 times, 1dtr into st before next sp, 6dtr into 11th sp, 1dc into 3rd acorn centre, 5dtr into next sp, 3dtr into st before next sp, 5dtr into next sp, 1dc into next acorn centre, 7dtr into last sp, 1dc into single loop at base ch corner.

Work a row of dc into single loops at base ch edge.

Complete opp sides to match, ending with 1ss.

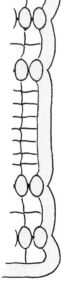

14 spaces and 4 'acorns' are formed along the shorter sides of the table runner

PURSE

✳

🍀 *Quickly made, this dainty purse with its shamrock emblem would make a nice gift – perhaps as a memento for 17 March, St Patrick's Day.*

MATERIALS

1 ball = approx 50–60g (2–2½oz)
Twilleys Southern Comfort Crochet Cotton
(3 ply: ball = 363/411m [400/450yd])
Optional 2nd colour for cord
Hook 2.00
2 beads with fairly large holes for threading onto cord ends
Embroidery needle
Green embroidery silk
Sewing needle and thread

TENSION

19sts and 21 rounds = 10cm (4in)

MEASUREMENTS

9 × 8·5cm (3½ × 3¼in)

METHOD

Starting at base, make 64ch. Join with ss into circle. Work 1dc, under top loop only, into each ch st for 1st round, and 1dc into top back loop of each foll dc, until 7cm (2¾in) from base. (Follow slanting line of sts from slip-knot to indicate where to end.)

EYELETS

*Make 2ch, miss next 2sts, 1dc (both loops) into each of next 2sts.
Rep from * to end. Replace the missed dc on next round by working 2dc into each 2ch sp, and cont in dc (top back loops) on the 64sts for another 0·75cm (⅓in). Work 1ss under both loops into next st.

EDGING

Round 1: *4ch, miss next 3sts, 1ss (both loops) into next st.
Rep from * ending with 1ss into base of 1st 4ch.
Round 2: Work 6dc into each 4ch sp. Ss into 1st dc. Break yarn and fasten off.

CORD

Make 160ch. Work back along ch with 1ss into 2nd and each foll single horizontal loop behind each st. Sew in all ends.

Turn purse to WS and flatten, with slip-knot at side. Join yarn to side of base and close base with ss through both edges, but work into 4 only alternate pairs of sts at each side (to gather), and into each rem pair.

Embroider small shamrock on one side (see right). Thread cord through eyelets. Fit beads onto cord ends and stitch in place.

Embroider the shamrock design onto the purse using the illustration as a guide to shape

FLOWERPOT COVER

✳ ✳

Even if you aren't lucky enough to have green fingers, you can work this lovely floral gift to cover a flowerpot on a windowsill or sideboard.

MATERIALS

50g (2oz) DMC Cebelia No 10 in main colour (MC) (sufficient for a 13.5cm (5½in) high pot with base and top dias of 12.5cm (5in) and 13.5cm (5½in)).
1 or more contrasting colours (CC) for stems, leaves and flowers
Hook 1.75
Matching sewing thread
Sewing needle

METHOD

Make a ch with MC to fit, slightly stretched, around base of pot. Join the untwisted ch into a circle with 1ss.

Round 1: Work 3ch for 1st tr, 1tr into each foll ch to end, 1ss into top of 1st tr. (For 12.5cm (5in) dia pot base = approx 126ch/126tr.)

Cont in rounds of tr to one round above height of pot. Fit cover onto pot every now and then and make gradual increases, in varying positions, as necessary.

Fold final round back onto outside, over prev round.

Make 1ch, and work an edging round of dc, inserting hook through both sps between trs of last 2 rounds. Work 1ss at end and fasten off.

STEMS

Measure the circumference around top of pot, and make two ch lengths in CC each half this measurement.

Make 4 of each size leaf for a larger pot, and 4 small and 4 medium for a small pot.

SMALL LEAF

Make 12ch in CC, 1dc into 2nd ch from hook, 1htr into each of next 4ch, 2htr into each of next 2ch, 1htr into each of next 3ch, 1dc into end ch.

Make 1ch, place slip-knot yarn end behind, then beg and ending with the 1dc, work back along base ch, following instructions in reverse (ie 1dc, 3htr, etc). Ss at end into missed ch at tip.

Break yarn and fasten off. Sew in ends.

MEDIUM LEAF

Make 14ch in CC, 1dc into 2nd ch from hook, 1htr into each of next 2ch, 1tr into each of next 3ch, 2tr into each of next 2ch, 1tr into each of next 3ch, 1htr into next ch, 1dc into end ch.

Make 1ch, place slip-knot yarn end behind, then beg and ending with the 1dc, work back along base ch, following instructions in reverse (ie 1dc, 1htr,

3tr, etc). Ss at end into missed ch at tip.
Break yarn and fasten off. Sew in ends.

◆

LARGE LEAF

Make 16ch in CC, 1dc into 2nd ch from hook, 1htr into next ch, 1tr into each of next 2ch, 1dtr into each of next 3ch, 2dtr into each of next 2ch, 1dtr into each of next 3ch, 1tr into next ch, 1htr into next ch, 1dc into end ch.

Make 1ch, place slip-knot yarn end behind, then beg and ending with the 1dc, work back along base ch, following instructions in reverse (ie 1dc, 1htr, 1tr, etc). Ss at end into missed ch at tip.
Break yarn and fasten off. Sew in ends.

◆

FLOWERS

For a small flowerpot, make only 2 small flowers: a larger pot requires 2 of each, where 1 complete flower is made by placing the small flower over the larger one.

For a large flower, make 6ch in CC. Join with ss into circle.

Round 1: 1ch, 12dc into circle, ss into 1st dc.

Round 2: 1ch, 1dc into same place as ch, 2dc into each rem st, ss into 1st ch.

Round 3: *7ch, 1dc into 2nd ch from hook, 1dc into each rem ch, 1dc into next dc on circle.
Rep from * working last dc into 1st of 7ch.

For a smaller flower, work as large flower to end Rnd1, then rep Rnd 3 but working 5ch instead of 7ch petals. Sew in all ends. Retain a slight point at tip of leaves.

Appliqué two similar designs of leaf and stem on each half of cover using sewing thread. Start with one stem approx 5cm (2in) from rim and ending approx 3cm (1½in) from base. (Begin the second stem a few cms before end of first stem.) Attach flowers by stitching around centre circles, leaving petals free. Make design according to pot size, using illustration as a rough guide (see below).

*The illustration shows the smaller flower placed over the larger,
the stem and one pair each of small, medium and large leaves*

SHAWL

*

A very straightforward method of increasing creates the long, triangular shape of this lovely old-fashioned shawl.

•

MATERIALS

350g (12½oz) Sirdar Country Style DK Yarn
Hook 5.00

•

TENSION

7htr/7sps and 12 rows = 10cm (4in)sq

•

MEASUREMENTS

(Excluding fringe) across top 1.5m (59in);
centre length 85cm (33½in); sides 113cm (44in)

•

METHOD

Starting at base point, make 6ch and join with ss into circle.

Row 1: 5ch, into circle work (1htr, 2ch) twice and 1htr, turn. (3sps).

Row 2: 5ch, (1htr, 2ch) into each of 1st 2 sps, (1htr, 2ch, 1htr) into last sp, turn. (4sps).

Row 3: 5ch, (1htr, 2ch) into each sp to last sp, (1htr, 2ch, 1htr) into last sp, turn. (5sps).

Rep last row until 99sps across top.

Do not turn – cont by working along 2 sides: 1ss into sp of last loop worked, 6ch (tr+3ch), 1htr into next 5ch loop, 3ch, 1tr into next htr loop, 3ch.

Work this patt, with (1htr, 3ch) into each 5ch loop and (1tr, 3ch) into each htr loop, along both sides of shawl. At base point work (1tr, 3ch) twice into the 6ch circle. Turn.

Cont with two more rows, but work only (1htr, 3ch) into each loop, (1tr, 3ch) twice into new base loop, and (1htr, 3ch) twice into final loop of 1st row. Omit last 3ch of 2nd row.

Break yarn and fasten off.

Cut 40cm (16in) lengths of yarn for fringe. Fold 5 of these together at centre (4 strands can be used, but the finished effect will not be as dense), insert fold into a 3ch loop on the shawl and thread ends through. Pull ends to make a fairly tight knot.

Rep for all 3ch loops. Trim ends.

BAG

**

This highly-textured handbag or small shopping bag is very pretty for summertime and functional, too.

•

MATERIALS

200g (7¼oz) Twilleys No1 Handicraft Cotton (DK)
Hook 4.50
Large press-stud
Matching sewing thread
Sewing needle
Lining fabric (optional)
2 × 28cm (11in) (approx) pieces of dowelling or cane (optional)

•

TENSION

Over tr st – 14sts and 7½ rows = 10cm (4in)sq

•

MEASUREMENTS

30cm (12in) sq

•

METHOD

Two pieces alike.

Make 45ch.

Row 1: 1tr into 4th ch from hook, 1tr into each foll ch to end, turn.

Row 2: 3ch (1st st), 1tr into each foll st to end, turn. (43sts in Rows 1–8).

Row 3: 2ch (1st st). With hook horizontal, work 1tr in front and around 2nd and each foll tr of last row, turn (see below).

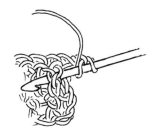

*Hook placement for 'tr around tr',
beginning at Row 3*

Row 4: 2ch (1st st). Work 1tr into 2nd and each foll tr of Row 2, working final tr into same st as last 2ch, turn.

Row 5: As Row 3, working final tr around 1st st of last row, turn.

Row 6: 2ch (1st st). Work 1tr into 2nd and each foll tr of Row 4, working final tr into same st as last 2ch, turn.

Row 7: As Row 3, working final tr around 1st st of last row, turn.

Row 8: 2ch (1st st). Work 1tr into 2nd and each foll tr of Row 6, working final tr into same st as last 2ch, turn.

Row 9: 2ch (1st st), (1tr,2ch,1dc) into 2nd st, * miss next 2sts, (1tr,2ch,1dc) into next st.

Shawl (page 23); Ladies' Gloves (page 26) and Bag (page 23)

Rep from * to last tr and 2ch start of prev row, miss 1tr, 1htr into top of 2ch, turn.

Row 10: 2ch (1st st), (1tr, 2ch, 1dc) into 1st 2ch sp, *(1tr, 2ch, 1dc) into next 2ch sp.

Rep from * to last 2sts, miss 1st, 1htr into last st, turn.

Rows 11–14: Rep last row 4 times more.

Row 15: 3ch, 1tr into 1st dc, *1tr into next 2ch sp, 1tr into each of next 2sts.

Rep from * to last 2ch sp, 1tr into sp, miss next st, 1tr into last st, turn. (43sts).

Rep Rows 2–6, Rows 9–15 and Rows 2–8.

Break yarn and fasten off. With the rows of bag running vertically, sew together base and 2 sides.

HANDLES

Using yarn doubled, make 4 × 10ch pieces for handle loops. Stitch at open edge: one piece to 1st and 3rd tr 'stripes' and another to 6th and 8th stripes on one side of bag. Rep for 2nd side. Sew in all ends. Make a handle using double ch st with 10m (33ft) of yarn. Thread through 2 loops on lhs and 2 loops on rhs of bag. Join into circle. Machine-stitch loop ends and handle-join for added strength if wished. Line if required. If using dowelling or cane, leave lining hems open at one end for removal before laundering.

Sew press-stud at centre, near to top of bag.

LADIES' GLOVES

❋ ❋

A silky-look yarn and small open pattern give these gloves a luxurious feel.

MATERIALS

100g (3¾oz) Twilleys Galaxia 5 (3 ply)
Hook 2.00
Sewing needle

TENSION

1dc, 3ch patt worked 12 times
+ 1dc = 12cm (4¾in) across
12 rows = 3cm (1¼in)

MEASUREMENTS

To fit average-sized hands

METHOD

Starting with back of left-hand glove at 4th finger side, make 93ch.

Row 1: 1dc into 9th ch from hook, *3ch, miss next 3ch, 1dc into next ch.

Rep from * to end, turn.

Row 2: 4ch (dc+3ch), *miss next 3ch, 1dc into next dc, 3ch.

Rep from * to last loop, miss 3ch, 1dc into next st, turn.

Rows 3–6: Rep last row 4 times more.

Row 7: 4ch, miss next 3ch, 1dc into next dc, (3ch, 1dc into next dc) 14 times. Make 40ch for 3rd finger.

Row 8: 1dc into 9th ch from hook, (3ch, miss next 3ch, 1dc into next ch) 7 times, 3ch.

Work the patt (Row 2 from *) to end, turn.

Rows 9–14: Rep Row 2, 6 times more.

Row 15: 4ch, 1dc into next dc, (3ch, 1dc into next dc) 15 times. Make 40ch for 2nd finger.

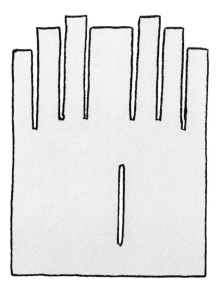

Outline shape for main section of glove

Row 16: As Row 8.

Rows 17–22: Rep Row 2, 6 times more.

Row 23: As Row 15 but make 36ch for 1st finger.

Row 24: 1dc into 9th ch from hook, (3ch, miss next 3ch, 1dc into next ch) 6 times, 3ch, miss next 3ch.

Patt to end, turn**.

Rows 25–36: Rep Row 2, 12 times more.

Row 37: 4ch, 1dc into next dc, (3ch, 1dc into next dc) 3 times, make 31ch, miss next 7dc, 1dc into next dc.

Patt to end, turn.

Row 38: As patt – work the (3ch, 1dc) patt along the 31ch.

Rows 39–40: Patt 2 more rows.

Rows 41 and 42: Rep Rows 15 and 8.

Rows 43–48: Patt 6 rows.

Row 49: Rep Row 15 but make 36ch for 3rd finger.

Row 50: Rep Row 24.

Rows 51–6: Patt 6 rows.

Row 57: Rep Row 7 but make 32ch for 4th finger.

Row 58: 1dc into 9th ch from hook, (3ch, miss next 3ch, 1dc into next ch) 5 times, 3ch, miss next 3ch.

Patt to end.

Rows 59–63: Patt 5 rows.

Break yarn and fasten off. Sew in ends.

RIGHT-HAND GLOVE

Work as for left glove to **, then rep Row 2 twice and Rows 37 and 38 once.

Patt 12 rows.

Cont from Row 41 to end.

Fold gloves, matching fingers, with RS inside. When wearing completed gloves, wrist edges will slightly curl onto wrists, although either side of fabric could be chosen as RS.

SIDE AND FINGER JOINING

(Note: Along any ch st edges, work into dc on nearest row.)

Beg at open side at wrist, join yarn to 1st st on 1st (nearest) side and work 1ch. Insert hook into 1st st on 2nd (furthest) side, yrh, draw loop through 2nd side, yrh, draw through both loops on hook to complete 1dc. Work 3ch, 1dc into next dc on 1st side, insert hook into next (equivalent) st on 2nd side, completing 1dc as before, 3ch. Cont along side, ending with 3ch and without working last corner dc. Gather top by working 3dc evenly across top of finger. Cont joining as on side until both dc at 4th finger base have been worked together. Make 1dc into dc at base of 3rd finger on 1st side and 1dc into base on 2nd side, 3ch.

Seam all fingers in the same way. Work 1ch at finish to secure.

Break yarn and fasten off. Sew in ends.

THUMB

This is made separately.

Make 28ch.

Row 1: 1dc into 8th ch from hook, *3ch, miss next 3ch, 1dc into next ch.

Rep from * to end, turn.

Row 2: 4ch, miss next 3ch, 1dc into next dc.

Patt to end, turn.

Row 3: 11ch, 1dc into 8th ch from hook, 3ch, miss next 3ch, 1dc into next dc.

Patt to end, turn.

Rows 4–7: Rep last 2 rows twice more. (12 loops).

Rows 8–11: Rep Row 2, 4 times more.

Row 12: Patt to last 2 loops, turn.

Row 13: 4ch, miss next 3ch, 1dc into next dc.

Patt to end, turn.

Rep last 2 rows twice more.

Break yarn, gather short, straight edge for top of thumb, and sew in ends.

Fold thumb RS inside. Seam 6-loop side using the 3ch, 1dc method. Ease into palm opening and stitch to WS glove allowing a small overlap at thumb base. Turn to RS.

Rep for 2nd thumb.

CHAPTER TWO

The Living Room

SOFA THROWOVER

✳

🍀 *Yarn from unpicked sweaters can be recycled to make a wide range of attractive crochet items, by combining these 'Granny' squares in different ways. The number of squares used in this traditional sofa throwover can be adjusted to fit any size of sofa or armchair.*

◆

MATERIALS
DK Yarn
Hook 4.00 or 4.50
Wool needle

◆

METHOD

If re-using yarn, wind it into skeins around the arms or back of a chair. Remove, and hold tautly (and very carefully!) over a boiling kettle spout to flatten the wrinkles.

Instead of working a round or rounds in one colour, make more interesting patterns by varying the colours of the 3tr forming each cluster. When changing colour, work the final (3rd) stage of a tr stitch with the next colour to be used, and twist colours on WS every few stitches as the work progresses.

Join completed squares with dc on RS using one colour only, and finish with a border of one or more rounds of dc.

To reduce the number of ends to be darned in, the pattern below uses 3ss to take a colour to the first cluster of a new round.

◆

METHOD FOR INDIVIDUAL SQUARES

Make 4ch. Join with ss into circle.

Round 1: 3ch (1st tr), 2tr into circle, 2ch, (3tr into circle, 2ch) 3 times, ss into top of 3ch.

Work 1ss into each of next 2sts, 1ss into next sp.

Round 2: 3ch (1st tr), (2tr, 2ch, 3tr) into same sp, * 1ch, (3tr, 2ch, 3tr) into next sp.

Rep from * twice more. 1ch, ss into top of 3ch, 2ss, 1ss into next sp.

Round 3: 3ch, (1st tr), (2tr, 2ch, 3tr) into same corner sp, *1ch, 3tr into next side sp, 1ch, (3tr, 2ch, 3tr) into next corner sp.

Rep from * twice more, 1ch, 3tr into next side sp, 1ch, ss into top of 3ch, 2ss, 1ss into next sp.

Round 4: 3ch (1st tr), (2tr, 2ch, 3tr) into same corner sp, *(1ch, 3tr into next side sp) twice, 1ch, (3tr, 2ch, 3tr) into next sp.

Rep from * twice more, 1ch, (3tr into next sp, 1ch) twice, ss into top of 3ch.

🍀

ANTIMACASSAR

✳ ✳

🍀 *Matching crocheted circles in three sizes are placed in such a way as to make a very pretty edging to this chairback cover.*

◆

MATERIALS
50g (2oz) DMC Cebelia No 20 Crochet Cotton
Hook 1.50
Linen union 44 × 62cm (17½ × 25in)
without selvedge

Matching sewing thread
Sewing needle
Embroidery needle

◆

TENSION

Work to complete circles 1, 2 and 3 to equal
9.5, 8 and 5.75 cm (3¾, 3¼ and 2in)
respectively

◆

OVERALL MEASUREMENTS
74 × 40cm (29 × 16in)

INDIVIDUAL CIRCLES

Circle 1: approx 9.5cm (3¾in) dia. Make 5

Make 4ch. Join with ss into circle.

Round 1: 4ch (1st dtr), 1dtr into circle, 3ch, (2dtr into circle, 3ch) 5 times, ss into top of 4ch.

Round 2: Ss between 1st 2dtr, 4ch (1st dtr), (1dtr,2ch,2dtr) into same sp, 3ch, miss next 3ch, * (2dtr,2ch,2dtr) into next dtr pair, 3ch, miss next 3ch. Rep from * to end, ss into top of 4ch.

Round 3: Ss between 1st 2dtr, 4ch (1st dtr), 1dtr into same sp, 4ch, miss next 2ch, *2dtr into next dtr pair, 4ch, miss next 2ch/3ch.
Rep from * to end, ss into top of 1st 4ch. (12 dtr pairs.)

Round 4: Ss between 1st 2dtr, 4ch (1st dtr), (1dtr,3ch,2dtr) into same sp, 3ch, miss next 4ch, * (2dtr,3ch,2dtr) into next dtr pair, 3ch, miss next 4ch. Rep from * to end, ss into top of 4ch.

Round 5: Ss between 1st 2dtr, 3ch (1st tr), 1tr into same sp, 2htr into next 3ch sp, 2tr into next dtr pair, 3tr into next 3ch sp, *2tr into next dtr pair, 2htr into next 3ch sp, 2tr into next dtr pair, 3tr into next 3ch sp.
Rep from * to end, ss into top of 1st 3ch. (108sts).

Round 6: 1ch (1st dc). Work 1dc into each foll st to end, ss into 1st dc.

Round 7: *4ch, miss next 2dc, 1ss into next dc.
Rep from * to end, working last ss into 1st 4ch base.

Round 8: 2ss along 1st ch loop, 1ss into 1st ch loop sp, *5ch, 1ss into next ch loop sp.
Rep from * to end, working last ss into 1st 5ch base.
Break yarn and fasten off. Sew in ends.

Circle 2: approx 8cm (3¼in) dia. Make 2

Rounds 1–3: Work as for Circle 1.

Round 4: Ss between 1st 2dtr, 3ch (1st tr), 1tr into same sp, 5htr into next 4ch sp, *2tr into next dtr pair, 5htr into next 4ch sp.
Rep from * to end, ss into top of 3ch. (84sts).
Rep Rnds 6,7 and 8 of Circle 1.
Break yarn and fasten off. Sew in ends.

Circle 3: approx 5.75cm (2in) dia. Make 7

Rounds 1 and 2: Work as for Circle 1.

Round 3: Ss between 1st 2dtr, 3ch (1st tr), 1tr into same sp, 2htr into next 2ch sp, 2tr into next dtr

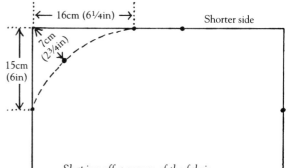

Shaping off a corner of the fabric

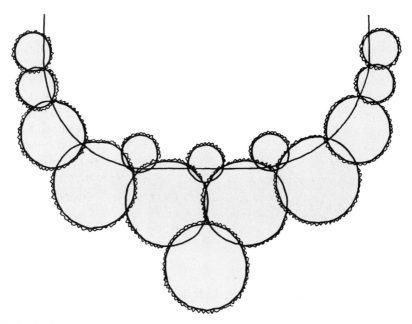

Arrangement of circles for the antimacassar

pair, 3htr into next 3ch sp, *2tr into next dtr pair, 2htr into next 2ch sp, 2tr into next dtr pair, 3htr into next 3ch sp.

Rep from * to end, ss into top of 3ch. (54 sts).

Rep Rnds 6,7 and 8 of Circle 1.

Break yarn and fasten off. Sew in ends.

SHAPING END OF FABRIC

From one corner, make a mark at 15cm (6in) on one longer side, and 16cm (6¼in) on shorter side (see page 34, top). Diagonally and centrally from corner, mark 7cm (2¾in). Cut out gentle curve between the 3 marks. Cut 2nd corner at same end to match. Make a 1cm (½in) hem all around fabric edge.

ASSEMBLING CIRCLES

Arrange circles as in diagram, or as desired, and sew together where they overlap each other (see page 34, below). Stitch down the edges that lie on the fabric, and invisibly along hem line.

With RS facing and with end circle on rhs, edge remainder of cover with 4ch loops (1dc between) of equal size to those on 7th rnd of circle. Insert hook through fabric, close to fold. At end, change to 5ch (1dc between), and incorporate outside edge only of circles.

Embroider chain st with same crochet cotton at 0.75cm (⅓in) from edge, around 3 straight sides.

PICTURE FRAME

✳✳✳

A lacy, antique frame – just what's needed to set off a very special picture.

MATERIALS

20g (1oz) DMC Cordonnet Special No 10 Crochet Cotton
Hook 1.75
To mount, you will need:
2 pieces stiff card: 20 × 24cm (8 × 9½in)
25cm (10in)sq piece of fabric, suitable for covering front of frame
Oddment of lining fabric
Medium iron-on interfacing (optional)
All-purpose adhesive
Spray adhesive for crochet reverse only
Scissors
Craft knife
Oddment of narrow ribbon for hanging

TENSION/MEASUREMENTS

Approx (outer) 19 × 16cm (7½ × 6¼in);
(inner) 13 × 10cm (5¼ × 4in)

METHOD

With crochet cotton and hook, make 184ch. Join with ss into untwisted circle.

Round 1: 1ch (1st dc), 1dc into each of next 37ch, 3dc into next ch (for corner), 1dc into each of next 51ch, 3dc into next ch, 1dc into each of next 39ch, 3dc into next ch, 1dc into each of next 51ch, 3dc into next ch, 1dc into next ch, ss into 1st dc.

Round 2: 1ch (1st dc), *miss next 2dc, (5tr into next dc, miss next 2dc, 1dc into next dc, miss next 2dc) to next corner, 9tr into corner st, miss next 2dc, 1dc into next dc.

Rep from * omitting last dc at end of round, ss into 1st dc.

Round 3: Ss to 3rd of lst 5tr, 6ch, *(1dc into 3rd of next 5tr grp, 5ch) to next 9tr corner, (1dc into 3rd of 9tr, 11ch, 1dc into 7th of 9tr, 5ch) into corner.
Rep from * to end, ss into 1st of 6ch.

Round 4: 7ch, 1htr into next dc, *5tr into 3rd of next 5ch, 1htr into next dc, (5ch, 1htr into next dc, 5tr into 3rd of next 5ch, 1htr into next dc) to next 11ch corner, 5tr into 3rd ch. Into 6th ch, work (1ss,3ch,1ss), 5tr into 9th ch, 1htr into next dc.
Rep from * to last 5ch, 5tr into 3rd of 5ch, ss into 2nd of 7ch.

Round 5: 3ch, *1tr into next htr, work a picot (=2ch, 1dc into last tr made), (1tr,picot) into each of next 5tr, 1tr into next htr.
Rep from * to next (5tr,3ch,5tr) corner, miss 1st 5tr.
Into 3ch sp, work (1ttr,picot) 9 times and 1ttr once, miss 2nd 5tr grp.

Rep from * until all 4 corners are worked, 1tr into next htr, picot, (1tr, picot) into each of next 5tr, ss into 3rd of 1st 3ch.

Break yarn and fasten off. Sew in ends.

◆

MOUNT

1 Lay crochet frame onto one piece of card and cut out a rectangle approx 0.5cm (¼in) larger all round than widest parts of the crochet. Cut out another rectangle the same size from the second piece of card.

2 Lay crochet onto one piece of card (front). Draw and cut out a window from the centre of the card, 3mm (⅛in) smaller all round than inner measurement of frame.

3 From card offcuts, make 3 × 1cm (½in) wide strips for spacers, 2 to fit down each side of card and 1 to sit in between them along base edge of frame. Glue spacers to outer edge on WS of card front.

4 To cover front of frame, position RS card front onto WS main fabric. Leaving approx 2cm (¾in) margin all round outer edge of fabric (for folding to WS), cut out rectangle. Iron on interfacing to WS of fabric, if used.

5 Cut off a triangle from each fabric corner, approx 1cm (½in) from card corners. Fold and glue all edges of fabric to WS of card. Allow to dry.

6 Make a window in the fabric by cutting a rectangle 2cm (¾in) smaller all round than inside edges of frame.

Diagonally snip corners of fabric window into corners of card window. Fold excess fabric to WS of card and glue down.

Apply additional glue to any fraying edges.

7 To help the picture slide in more easily, cut a picture frame from lining fabric approx 0.5cm (¼in) smaller than frame, and glue onto WS of front.

8 On card back, make a tiny slit 3cm (1¼in) from centre top. Insert a small ribbon loop for hanging. Glue ends to WS.

9 Apply glue along edges only to top and 2 sides of WS back, and affix to front.

10 Using spray adhesive, attach crochet frame to fabric.

'Windows' Cushion (page 38); Antimacassar (page 33); Small Blanket (page 38)

SMALL BLANKET

✻

Always useful on cool evenings, this stripy little blanket is perfect for tucking over knees while playing cards or relaxing before bed.

◆

MATERIALS

200g (7¼oz) each of colours A and B, Jarol Supersaver DK Yarn
Hook 6.00
Wool needle

◆

TENSION

16dc and 20 rows = 11cm (4¼in)sq

◆

MEASUREMENTS

Approx 77 × 105cm (30 × 41in)

◆

METHOD

The blanket is worked in strips of double crochet, sewn together.
With col A make 17ch.

Row 1: 1dc into 2nd ch from hook, 1dc into each foll ch to end, turn.
Row 2: 1ch (1st dc), 1dc into each foll st to end, turn. (16sts).
Form a square by repeating last row 18 times more. Change to next colour when working the dc at end of final row by drawing through new colour to start next row.
Work 20 rows with col B.
Cont alternating colours every 20 rows until the work is 9 sqs in length. Start next strip with col B and so on, so that a pattern of checks is formed with 7 strips.
Place the flat of 2 strips together, matching dc 'stripes'. Oversew along edge. When all strips are joined, work 4ch loops with either colour yarn along each shorter edge – 5 loops across each square. Sew in ends.
Make a fringe by knotting 4 × 20cm (8in) long strands of yarn into each loop. Use col A next to a col B square, and col B next to a col A square.

'WINDOWS' CUSHION

✻✻

The 'window' panels worked on the front of this cushion could be backed with the same or toning furnishing fabrics as the room it is intended for, to create a sophisticated, designer look.

◆

MATERIALS

250g (9oz) Twilleys Secco No 3 Cotton (4 ply)
Hook 3.50
35cm (13½in) sq furnishing fabric
Approx 35cm (13½in) sq inner cushion
Matching sewing thread
Sewing needle
Touch-and-close fastening or zip
(optional)

◆

TENSION

20dc and 20 rows = 10cm (4in)sq

◆

FRONT

Make 78ch.
Row 1: (RS)1dc into 2nd ch from hook, 1dc into each foll ch to end, turn.
Row 2: 2ch (1st st), 1dc into front top loop of next (2nd) st, *1dc into back top loop of next st, 1dc into front top loop of next st.
Rep from * to last st, 1dc into both loops, turn. (77sts).
Rep last row until 6cm (2¼in) has been worked, ending with RS facing for next row.

RIGHT-HAND BORDER

2ch (1st st). Retaining patt, work 1dc into each of next 11sts, 1dc (both loops) into next st, turn.
Rep last row until approx 16cm (6¼in) from base ch, ending at inside edge. Break yarn and fasten off.

VERTICAL BAR OF CROSS

With RS facing, rejoin yarn to 23rd st from 13sts of RH border (ie 36th st from rhs). Make 2ch (1st st). Retaining patt, but working 1dc into back top loop for the 2nd st of each row, work 1dc into each of next 6sts.
Cont patt on these 7sts until vertical bar of cross equals length of RH border.
End at lhs with RS facing. Break yarn and fasten off.

LEFT-HAND BORDER

With RS still facing, rejoin yarn to 13th st from lhs. 2ch (1st st).
Retaining patt (as Row 2 of Front), work to end, turn.
Cont patt of these 13sts until LH border equals length of RH border.
End at outside edge. Turn.

HORIZONTAL BAR OF CROSS

Next Row: 2ch (1st st), patt next 12sts, make 22ch, 1dc into front top loop of 1st of 7 centre sts, 1dc into back top loop of next st. Patt next 5sts, make 22ch, 1dc into back top loop of 1st of 13 RH border sts, patt to end, turn.
Next Row: 2ch (1st st), patt to 1st 22ch, 1dc into each ch st, 1dc into front top loop of 1st of 7 centre sts, patt next 6sts, 1dc into each of next 22ch, 1dc into back top loop of 1st of next 13sts, patt to end. (77sts)**.
Rep Row 2 of front until length of horizontal bar and width of vertical bar of cross are fairly equal, and ending with RS facing for next row.
Work RH and LH borders, and vertical bar of cross, as before, so that 4 fairly square 'windows' will be formed.
Rep from ** to ** once more.
Cont until lengths of both top and bottom borders are equal. Break yarn and fasten off.

BACK

Work as front until end of Row 2.

Rep Row 2 until lengths of back and front are equal. Break yarn and fasten off.
With RS of front facing, work 21dc – or adjust as necessary – along vertical sides of each window. Sew in all ends.

PANEL

Make 79ch.
Row 1: 1dtr into 11th ch from hook, *3ch, miss next 3ch, 1dtr into next ch. Rep from * to end, turn. (18sqs).
Work to a tension of 7 × 7sqs = window opening.
Row 2: 7ch (dtr+3ch), 1dtr into next dtr, *3ch, miss next 3ch, 1dtr into next dtr.
Rep from * to end, turn.
Rep last row until 18sqs in length.
Break yarn and fasten off.
Stitch panel behind front openings, concealing 2 lines of sqs behind vertical and horizontal bars of cross – attach edge dtrs just behind window edges.
Stitch outer edges of panel to WS of front.

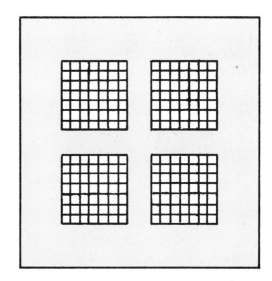

Completed cushion front, showing four 'windows'

Trim fabric 2cm (¾in) larger all round than 18sq panel, rounding off corners. Oversew edge to prevent fraying. Turn under 1cm (⅜in) all round onto RS, place RS of fabric centrally against WS of panel and stitch down edge.
On RS, join cushion back and front along 3 sides with even dc, increasing as necessary at corners – leave base ch side open.
Insert inner cushion, loosely oversew open edges together, or affix zip or touch-and-close fastening.

NEEDLECASE WITH PICOT CROCHET EDGE

❀❀

The arch shape was chosen to hold sewing needles of differing lengths. When designing the embroidery, use the shape as representation of a tunnel, window, or whatever takes your fancy, to create a personalised needlecase for yourself or to give as a gift.

•

MATERIALS

12.6 × 8cm (5 × 3¼in) piece of linen or any
suitable plain fabric
Lightweight lining fabric
Iron-on interfacing
Scrap of felt to hold needles
6-stranded embroidery silks in 2 or more colours
Hook 1.75
Matching sewing thread
Sewing needle
Embroidery needle

METHOD

1 Cut out both fabrics and interfacing as shown on page 42.

2 Cut the interfacing into 3 pieces – 2 arches and spine. Trim so that arched pieces are 0.5cm (¼in) smaller all round than fabric (each arch will be 5cm (2in) wide). The narrow, 0.5cm (¼in) strip remaining is for the 'spine', like a book cover.

3 Place RS of main fabric and lining together, tack, and stitch edges, excluding base, using 0.5cm (¼in) wide seam.

4 Trim round stitched edges and snip curves. Turn to RS and press.

5 Work some embroidery on the front using one or two strands of silks. Work into main fabric only.

6 Iron on the 3 pieces of interfacing to WS of main fabric, trimming the interfacing if necessary.

RIGHT: *Place Mat (page 42)*

CHAPTER THREE

The Kitchen

ICE CREAM BORDER

✳✳

A fun addition to any kitchen, these crocheted 'cones' with their cotton 'ice cream' will stimulate the appetite of children and adults alike!

MATERIALS

100g (3¾oz) Twilleys No1 Handicraft Cotton (DK)
Hook 4.00
Scissors
Cotton fabric for ice-cream appliqué
Matching sewing thread
Sewing needle
Medium iron-on interfacing
Thin card

TENSION

8cm (3in) across top × 15cm (6in)
long = 1 point (cone)

MEASUREMENTS

107 × 22cm (42 × 8½in) = 10 points
joined and completed

POINTS

Make 4ch.

Row 1: Miss 3ch, 1tr into 4th ch from hook, turn. (1st 3ch counts as 1st tr.)

Row 2: 3ch, 1tr into 1st st (top of tr of 1st row), 1tr into top of 3ch, turn. (3sts).

Row 3: 3ch, 1tr into 1st st, 1tr into each of next 2sts, turn. (4sts).

Row 4: 3ch, 1tr into 1st st, 1tr into each of next 3sts, turn. (5sts).

Cont inc of 1tr at beg of each row until 12 sts. Break yarn and fasten off.

Make 10 or as many points as required. Do not break yarn at end of last point. Turn.

HEADING

Row 1: Join points together as follows: 3ch, 1tr into 1st st, 1tr into each of rem 11sts.

Inc at start of each point as before, work 13tr across each rem point, (slip-knot ends at rhs), turn.

Rows 2–6: 3ch, 1tr into next and each foll st to end, turn.

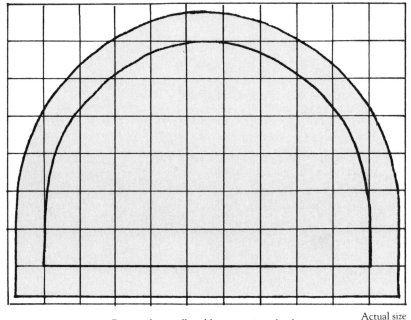

Pattern for small and large semi-circles for interfacing and fabric

Actual size

Row 7: 2ch, 1dc into 2nd st, *1ch, 1dc into next st.
Rep from * to end.
Break yarn and fasten off. Sew in ends.
Use diagram on page 46 to cut out the two semi-circles from card and use as templates. For each point, cut out the smaller semi-circle from interfacing and larger semi-circle from fabric.
Fuse interfacing onto fabric.
Turn in raw edges of fabric, tack, and appliqué onto valance (see right).

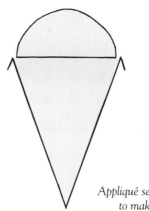

*Appliqué semi-circles above points
to make the 'ice-cream cones'*

COFFEE JAR COVER

✳

Instead of throwing away an empty coffee jar, transform it into a decorative and useful container by making this string mesh cover and hinged lid.

MATERIALS

Approx 50m (55 yd) thin cotton string
Hook 5.00
Large wool needle
All-purpose adhesive

TENSION

14½tr = 10cm (4in);
1st 2 rounds = 7cm (2¾in) dia

MEASUREMENTS

To fit (approx) 15.5cm high × 22cm circum
(6½ × 8in) (100g (3¾oz) jar)

COVER

Make 5ch. Join with ss into circle.
Round 1: 3ch (1st tr), 14tr into circle, ss into top of 3ch.
Round 2: 3ch, 1tr into same place as 3ch, *2tr into next tr.
Rep from * to end, ss into top of 3ch.
Rounds 3–5: 1ch (1st dc), 1dc into each foll st to end, ss into 1st dc.

Round 6: *2ch, miss next dc, 1dc into next dc.
Rep from * working last dc into 1st 2ch sp.
Round 7: 2ch, *1dc into next 2ch sp, 2ch.
Rep from * to end.
Place marker beneath last st and treat round ends as being vertically above marker.
Rounds 8–16: Beg with 1dc into next 2ch sp, rep last round 9 times more (or no of times necessary for cover to reach, when fully stretched, approx 3cm (1¼in) from jar rim).
Round 17: Work 2dc into each foll 2ch sp to end, ss into 1st dc.
Re-insert marker to indicate round ends.
Round 18: 1ch (1st dc), 1dc into each foll dc to end, ss into 1st dc.
Rounds 19–22: Rep last round 4 times more.
Break yarn, leaving a 25cm (10in) end for gathering. Fasten off.
Stretch cover over jar and gather top to fit inside rim, 2cm (¾in) down and around. Glue inside rim. Temporarily wedge a cardboard tube or similar inside to hold until glue is dry.

◆

LID

Make 140ch.
1dc into 2nd ch from hook, 1dc into each foll ch to end. Work 5ch, turn, and make 1ss into last dc made. Break yarn leaving a 40cm (16in) end.

Buttonhole-stitched handle at one end of dc strip

Around the 5ch, work a tight buttonhole st (see Techniques) with the end, into 5ch sp, for the handle (see above). Secure ends into WS of dc row. Beg at same end (RS outside and right way up), turn

handle, glueing and coiling the crochet strip tightly around handle base, ending up with a flat disc (jar-top size) with handle protruding from centre. Now shape a gentle upward slope towards centre (see below).

Completed shape of lid

Smear a little more glue onto underside of lid, and allow to dry.
Stitch 2 loose hinges between lid and cover.

EGG COSY

Start someone's day with a smile, with a cheerful egg cosy, perfect for using up oddments of yarn left over from other projects.

MATERIALS
DK Yarn oddments (2 colours)
Hooks 4.00; 3.50 for final round
Wool needle

TENSION
1st 2 rounds – 3.25cm (1¼in) dia (medium cosy)
3.5cm (1½in) dia (large cosy)

METHOD
With 1st col and 4.00 hook, make 3ch. Join with ss into circle.
Round 1: 2ch (1st htr), 7htr into circle.

Use small safety pin to indicate round ends.
Round 2: 2dc into each of 8htr.
Round 3: 1dc into each dc.
Round 4: *1dc into next dc, 2dc into foll dc. Rep from * to end. (24sts).
Rounds 5–9: As Rnd 3.
Round 10: 1ss into next dc, 2ch (1st htr), 1htr into each foll dc to end, ss into top of 2ch.
Round 11: 2ch (1st htr), 1htr into same place as 2ch, 2htr into each foll htr to end, ss into top of 2ch.
Round 12: 2ch (1st htr), 1htr into each foll htr to end, ss into top of 2ch.
Round 13: 1ch (1st dc), 1dc into each foll st to end, ss into 1st dc.
(Change to 2nd col and 3.50 hook.)
Round 14: As Rnd 13.
Work a round of ch st for 'hat' band using wool needle.

block of 4tr. (Last st of sq counts as 1st
st of next sq.)
For further instructions on filet crochet, see p11.

◆

METHOD

Make 54ch.
Row 1: 1tr into 4th ch from hook, 1tr into each of

next 5ch, (2ch, miss next 2ch, 1tr into next ch) 3
times, 1tr into each of next 3ch, (2ch, miss next
2ch, 1tr into next ch) 10 times, 1tr into each of next
3ch, turn.
Follow chart below from Row 2, working block inc
at beg of odd rows and block dec at end of even rows,
as shown. Patt repeats after Row 48.

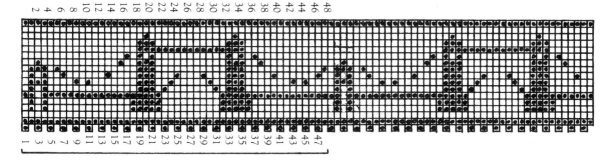

Chart for filet shelf edging (1 patt = 48 rows)

JUG COVER

✳✳✳

🍀 *This jug cover is simply a large doily with a
pretty pineapple pattern, to which muslin
and beads are attached.*

◆

MATERIALS

2 × 20g (1oz) Twilleys 20 Crochet Cotton
(2 colours)
Hook 1.25
Approx 20cm (8in) dia circle of laundered muslin
20 beads for edge of cover. These should be
fairly weighty without being too large – max
2cm (¾in) long
Matching sewing thread
Sewing needle

◆

MEASUREMENTS

Approx 25cm (10in) dia

◆

METHOD

Make 6ch. Join with ss into circle.
Work each round using colours alternately.
Round 1: 3ch (1st tr), 19tr into circle, ss into top of
3ch.

Round 2: 3ch, 1tr into same place as 3ch, 2ch, miss
next tr, *2tr into next tr, 2ch, miss next tr.
Rep from * to end, ss into top of 3ch. (10 pairs).
Round 3: 3ch, 1tr into same place as 3ch, 2ch, *2tr
into next tr, 2ch.
Rep from * to end, ss into top of 3ch.
Round 4: Ss into next 2ch sp, 3ch (1st tr),
(2tr,2ch,3tr) into same sp, 1ch, 1dc into next sp,
1ch,* (3tr,2ch,3tr = V grp) into next sp, 1ch, 1dc
into next sp, 1ch.
Rep from * to end, ss into top of 3ch.
Round 5: Ss into next 2ch sp, 7ch (tr+4ch), 1tr
into same sp, 3ch, V grp into next 2ch sp, 3ch,
*(1tr,4ch,1tr) into next 2ch sp, 3ch, V grp into
next 2ch sp, 3ch.
Rep from * to end, ss into 3rd of 7ch.
Round 6: 3ch (1st tr), 8tr into next 4ch sp, 3ch, V
grp into next 2ch sp, 3ch, *9tr into next 4ch sp,
3ch, V grp into next 2ch sp, 3ch.
Rep from * to end, ss into top of 1st 3ch.
Round 7: 3ch, (1dc into next tr, 3ch) 8 times, V
grp into next 2ch sp, 3ch, *(1dc into next tr of 9tr
grp, 3ch) 9 times, V grp into next 2ch sp, 3ch.
Rep from * to end.

Round 8: *(1dc into next 3ch sp between dcs, 3ch) 8 times, (V grp, 2ch, 3tr) into next 2ch sp, 3ch. Rep from * to end.

Round 9: *(1dc into next 3ch sp between dcs, 3ch) 7 times, (V grp, 3ch) into each of next 2 2ch sps. Rep from * to end.

Round 10: *(1dc into next 3ch sp between dcs, 3ch) 6 times, V grp into next 2ch sp, 3ch, (1tr, 4ch, 1tr) into next 3ch sp, 3ch, V grp into next 2ch sp, 3ch. Rep from * to end.

Round 11: *(1dc into next 3ch sp between dcs, 3ch) 5 times, V grp into next 2ch sp, 3ch, 8tr into next 4ch sp, 3ch, V grp into next 2ch sp, 3ch. Rep from * to end.

Round 12: *(1dc into next 3ch sp between dcs, 3ch) 4 times, V grp into next 2ch sp, 3ch, (1dc into next tr of 8tr grp, 3ch) 8 times, V grp into next 2ch sp, 3ch. Rep from * to end.

Round 13: *(1dc into next 3ch sp between dcs, 3ch) 3 times, (V grp, 2ch, 3tr) into next 2ch sp, 3ch, (1dc into next 3ch sp between dcs, 3ch) 7 times, (V grp, 2ch, 3tr) into next 2ch sp, 3ch. Rep from * to end.

Round 14: *(1dc into next 3ch sp between dcs, 3ch) twice, (V grp, 3ch) into each of next 2 2ch sps, (1dc into next 3ch sp between dcs, 3ch) 6 times, (V grp, 3ch) into each of next 2 2ch sps. Rep from * to end.

Round 15: *1dc into 3ch sp at next 'pineapple' top, 3ch, V grp into next 2ch sp, 3ch, 3tr into next 3ch sp, 3ch, V grp into next 2ch sp, 3ch, (1dc into next 3ch sp between dcs, 3ch) 5 times, V grp into next 2ch sp, 3ch, 3tr into next 3ch sp, 3ch, V grp into next 2ch sp, 3ch. Rep from * to end.

Round 16: Ss into next dc stem, 6ss to next 2ch sp, 1ss into sp. *3ch (1st tr), 2tr into same sp, 3ch, (3tr, 3ch) into each of next 2sps, V grp into next 2ch sp, 3ch, (1dc into next 3ch sp between dcs, 3ch) 4 times, V grp into next 2ch sp, 3ch, (3tr, 3ch) into each of next 3sps.

Replace 1st 3ch with 1tr, and rep from * – work 1st 3tr into next 2ch sp.

Ss into top of 1st 3ch.

RIGHT: *Filet Shelf Edging (page 50); Jug Cover (page 51); Filet Jam Pot Covers (page 50). Also shown are yellow gingham jug and jam pot covers which have crocheted picot edges (see Edgings, page 118)*
FAR RIGHT: *Basin Holders (page 54); Plant Hanging (page 55)*

Round 17: Ss into next 3ch sp, 3ch (1st tr), 2tr into same sp, 3ch, (3tr,3ch) into each of next 2 sps, *V grp into next 2ch sp, 3ch, (1dc into next 3ch sp between dcs, 3ch) 3 times, V grp into next 2ch sp, 3ch, (3tr,3ch) into each of next 7 sps.
Rep from * working last (3tr, 3ch) into only 4 sps at end of round, ss into top of 1st 3ch.

Rounds 18–19: Ss into next 3ch sp and cont patt, as set, for two more rounds.

Round 20: Ss into next 3ch sp, 3ch (1st tr), 2tr into same 3ch sp, 3ch. Work (3tr, 3ch) into each foll sp, missing over (3ch,1dc,3ch) above each of 5 outer pineapples.

Round 21: Cont patt, as set, to end but work V grp into next and every foll 3rd 3ch sp.
(If desired, use just one colour for last 2 rounds.)

Round 22: Patt, as set to end working V grp into each 2ch sp.

Round 23: Work only 2ch between each 3tr grp, continuing with the V grp into each 2ch sp.
Break yarn and fasten off.
Tack muslin circle centrally to WS of crochet cover.
Turn under edge and stitch.
Attach bead to each V grp.

BASIN HOLDERS

❋

Very useful at Christmas and other occasions, these openwork holders placed around pudding basins will help prevent burned fingers and ease the operation of lifting them from saucepans of boiling water. (Could also be made with suitable string.)

◆

MATERIALS

Twilleys No 1 Handicraft Cotton (DK)
– small quantity
Hook 4.00

Sketch to show working of first three rounds

◆

METHOD

Work first three rounds for the small basin holder (see below left), and four or five rounds for larger sizes.
Make 14ch. Join with ss into circle.

Round 1: *1dc into circle, 10ch.
Rep from * 4 times more. Even out sts around circle. 1ss into start of 1st 10ch.

Round 2: Ss to centre of same ch, 1ss into same 10ch sp, *16ch, 1dc into next 10ch sp.
Rep from * 3 times more, 16ch, 1ss into start of 1st 16ch.

Round 3: 21ch, 1dc into same (1st) 16ch sp, * 21ch, 1dc into centre of dc stem at end of this ch, 21ch, 1dc into next 16ch sp.
Rep from * 3 times more, 21ch, 1ss into start of lst 21ch.

Round 4: Ss to centre of same ch, 1ss into same 21ch sp, *16ch, 1dc into next 21ch sp.
Rep from * 8 times more, 16ch, 1ss into start of 1st 16ch.
Rep last round once more for larger holder, working into 16ch sps.
Fasten off.

◆

HANDLE

Make a double ch to an approx length of 75cm (30in) or 90cm (35in). Thread through outer loops and secure into a circle.

54

PLANT HANGING

❋❋

🍀 *The plant container is held in a honeycomb-pattern mesh between two sturdy rings covered in dc. The pattern is easily adapted for any size of basket.*

•

MATERIALS

2 × 50g (2oz) Twilleys Stalite Perlespun No 3 (4 ply)
40g (1¾oz) artificial raffia
Hooks 4.00 and 6.00
2 strong, narrow metal rings, 5cm (2in)
and 10cm (4in) dia
Wool needle
Lightweight basket – approx 25cm (10in) dia
× 9cm (3½in) high

METHOD

With Stalite and 4.00 hook, work approx 200dc around larger ring to conceal metal, making even-sized sts and not too tight. Break yarn and fasten off. Twist sts into a spiral, approx 24 times. Sew in ends, joining circle of sts.

To make the covering for the basket, use Stalite, doubled, and 6.00 hook.

Round 1: Work 48dc around smaller ring. Ss into 1st st.

Round 2: 4ch (1st tr + 1ch), miss next st, *1tr into next st, 1ch, miss next st.

Rep from * to end, ss into 3rd of 4ch, ss into next sp.

Round 3: 5ch (1st tr + 2ch), *1tr into next sp, 2ch.

Rep from * to end, ss into 3rd of 5ch, 1ch, ss into next sp.

Round 4: 6ch (1st tr + 3ch), *1tr into next sp, 3ch.

Rep from * to end, ss into 3rd of 6ch, 2ch, ss into next sp.

Rounds 5 and 6: 7ch (1st tr + 4ch), *1tr into next sp, 4ch.

Rep from * to end, miss 2ch, ss into 3rd of 7ch, 2ch, ss into next sp.

Rounds 7 and 8: 8ch (1st tr + 5ch), *1tr into next sp, 5ch.

Rep from * to end, miss 2ch, ss into 3rd of 8ch.
Fasten off and sew in ends.

For the 'strings', use the same hook and doubled yarn, and make a double ch, a little under 4¼m (14ft) in length. Leaving 20cm (8in) for stitching ends together, break yarn and fasten off. Weave string through outer loops of cover, and 4 times through larger ring (see below). If the strings have become twisted, smooth out. Overlap and secure ends well.

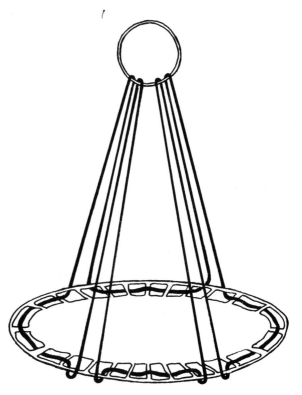

Weave braid through outer loops and four times through larger ring

With raffia and 6.00 hook, make 4 spirals, as follows: make 34ch. Into 2nd ch from hook, work (1dc, 1htr, 2tr), 4tr into each foll ch to last ch, (2tr, 1htr, 1dc) into last ch.

Tie ends into a small bow around 4 pairs of strings, approx 5cm (2in) up from loops.

Tablecloth (page 60); Traycloth (page 59); Lacy Doilies (page 58) shown in both blue and white

CHAPTER FOUR

Teatime

LACY DOILY

❋❋

Made in the finest cotton, this lovely lacy doily will certainly be treasured, and is the perfect complement to a bone china tea service.

◆

MATERIALS

20g (1oz) Coats Crochet Cotton No 20
(may require a little extra yarn if crocheted loosely)
Hook 1.25

◆

TENSION

1st 8 rounds = 9cm (3½in) dia

◆

MEASUREMENTS

Approx 27cm (10½in) dia

◆

METHOD

Make 7ch. Join with ss into circle.

Round 1: 3ch (1st st). Into circle work 1tr, 4ch, (2tr,4ch) 4 times, ss into top of 3ch. (5 loops).

Round 2: Ss to and into 1st loop, 3ch, (2tr,4ch,3tr) into same loop, 5ch, *(3tr,4ch,3tr) into next loop, 5ch.
Rep from * to end, ss into top of 3ch.

Round 3: Ss to and into 1st 4ch loop (=3ss), 3ch, (2tr,4ch,3tr) into same loop, 6ch, miss (3tr, 5ch and foll 3tr), *(3tr,4ch,3tr) into next 4ch loop, 6ch, miss (3tr,5ch and foll 3tr).
Rep from * to end, ss into top of 3ch.

Round 4: 3ss, 3ch, (2tr,4ch,3tr) into same loop, 10ch, *(3tr,4ch,3tr) into next 4ch loop, 10ch.
Rep from * to end, ss into top of 3ch.

Round 5: 2ss, 2ss into loop, 3ch, 2tr into same loop, *6ch, 1dc into 1st ch st of next 10ch, 12ch, 1dc under 3 loops below (enclosing 5ch, 6ch and 10ch of prev 3 rounds), 12ch, 1dc into last ch st of same 10ch of prev round, 6ch, 3tr into next 4ch loop.
Rep from * omitting last 3tr at end of round, ss into top of 3ch.

Round 6: 1ss into centre tr of 1st grp, 8ch, *miss next 6ch loop, 1dc into 1st of next 2 12ch loops, 7ch, 1dc into next 12ch loop, 7ch, miss next 6ch loop, 1dc into next centre tr, 7ch.

Rep from * omitting last (dc and 7ch) at end of round, ss into 1st of 8ch.

Round 7: 1ss into 1st 7ch loop, 2ch (1st st), 5htr into same loop, 4ch, *6htr into next 7ch loop, 4ch.
Rep from * to end, ss into top of 2ch.

Round 8: 3ch, 1tr into each of next 5htr, (1htr,1ch,1htr) into next 4ch loop, *1tr into each of next 6htr, (1htr,1ch,1htr) into next 4ch loop.
Rep from * to end, ss into top of 3ch.

Round 9: 8ss to and into next 1ch sp, 7ch, 1tr into same sp, 7ch, *(1tr,4ch,1tr) into next 1ch sp, 7ch.
Rep from * to end, ss into 3rd of 1st 7ch.

Round 10: 2ss into 1st 4ch loop, 7ch, 1tr into same loop, 3ch, *(1tr,4ch,1tr) into 4th of next 7ch, 3ch, (1tr,4ch,1tr) into next 4ch loop, 3ch.
Rep from * to end, ss into 3rd of 1st 7ch.

Round 11: 2ss into 1st 4ch loop, 7ch, 1tr into same loop, (1tr,4ch,1tr) into next 3ch loop, *(1tr,4ch,1tr) into next 4ch loop, (1tr,4ch,1tr) into next 3ch loop.
Rep from * to end, ss into 3rd of 7ch.

Round 12: 2ss into 1st 4ch loop, 7ch, 1tr into same loop, *(1tr,4ch,1tr) into next 4ch loop.
Rep from * to end, ss into 3rd of 7ch.

Rounds 13 and 14: Rep last round twice more.

Round 15: 1ss into 1st 4ch sp, 3ch, 3tr into same sp, *4tr into next 4ch sp.
Rep from * to end, ss into top of 3ch.

Round 16: *5ch, 1dc between next 2 4tr grps.
Rep from * to end. Do not ss. (60 loops).

Round 17: 2ss into 1st 5ch loop, 3ch, (2tr,4ch,3tr) into same loop, 3ch, 1dc into next loop, 14ch, miss next loop, 1dc into next loop, 3ch, *(3tr,4ch,3tr) into next loop, 3ch, 1dc into next loop, 14ch, miss next loop, 1dc into next loop, 3ch.
Rep from * to end, ss into top of 1st 3ch.

Round 18: 3ss, 3ch, (2tr,4ch,3tr) into same 4ch loop, 13ch, miss 3 loops, *(3tr,4ch,3tr) into next 4ch loop, 13ch, miss 3 loops.
Rep from * to end, ss into top of 3ch.

Round 19: 3ss, 3ch, (2tr,4ch,3tr) into same 4ch loop, 16ch, miss 13ch, *(3tr,4ch,3tr) into next 4ch loop, 16ch, miss 13ch.
Rep from * to end, ss into top of 3ch.

Round 20: 3ss, 3ch, (2tr,4ch,3tr) into same 4ch

loop, 17ch, miss 16ch, *(3tr,4ch,3tr) into next 4ch loop, 17ch, miss 16ch.

Rep from * to end, ss into top of 3ch.

Round 21: 2ss, 2ss into loop, 3ch, 2tr into same loop, *6ch, 1dc into 1st ch st of next 17ch, 13ch, 1dc under 4 loops below (enclosing 14ch, 13ch, 16ch and 17ch of prev 4 rounds), 13ch, 1dc into last ch st of same 17ch, 6ch, 3tr into next 4ch loop. Rep from * omitting last 3tr at end of round, ss into top of 3ch.

Round 22: 1ss into centre tr of 1st grp, 8ch, *miss next 6ch loop, 1htr into 1st of next 2 13ch loops,

7ch, 1htr into next 13ch loop, 7ch, miss next 6ch loop, 1dc into next centre tr, 7ch.

Rep from * omitting last (dc and 7ch) at end of round, ss into 1st of 8ch.

Round 23: 3ch, 2tr into last ss made, 3ch, 3tr into 1st 7ch loop, 3ch, *(3tr into next htr, 3ch, 3tr into next 7ch loop, 3ch) twice, "3tr into next dc, 3ch, 3tr into next 7ch loop, 3ch".

Rep from *, omitting " to " at end of round.

Round 24: 1ss into centre tr of 1st grp, 3ch, 2tr into last ss made, 3ch, * 3tr into next centre tr, 3ch.

Rep from * to end.

TRAYCLOTH

✳✳

Using sewing cotton for the final round of the border gives this diamond-patterned traycloth extra definition, especially if a strongly contrasting colour is chosen.

◆

MATERIALS

60g (2½oz) DMC Cordonnet Special No 10 Crochet Cotton
Sewing thread in contrasting colour
Hook 1.50

◆

TENSION

8½ loops = 10cm (4in) across

◆

MEASUREMENTS

49 × 34cm (19 × 13½in)

◆

METHOD

Make 153ch.

Row 1: 1dc into 9th ch from hook, *5ch, miss next 3ch, 1dc into next ch.

Rep from * to end, turn.

Row 2: 5ch, 1dc into 1st 5ch sp, *5ch, 1dc into next sp. Rep from * until all 37 loops have been worked into, 2ch, 1tr into 4th of last 8ch, turn.

Row 3: 5ch, miss next 2ch, *1dc into next 5ch sp, 5ch. Rep from * to last loop, miss 1st 2ch of loop, 1dc into next ch, turn.

Row 4: 5ch, 1dc into 1st 5ch sp, *5ch, 1dc into next sp.

Rep from * until all loops have been worked into, 2ch, 1tr into end ch, turn.

Row 5: (RS)5ch, miss next 2ch, 1dc into next sp, (5ch, 1dc) into each of next 2 sps, (5tr into next dc = fan), 1dc into next sp, *patt 5 (5ch,1dc) loops, fan, 1dc into next sp.

Rep from * to last 3 loops, patt 2 loops, 5ch, 1dc into 3rd of next 5ch, turn.

Row 6: As Row 4, but work 1dc into centre tr of each fan, where they occur.

Row 7: 5ch, miss next 2ch, 1dc into next sp, (patt 1 loop, fan, 1dc into next sp) twice, *patt 3 loops, fan, 1dc into next sp, patt 1 loop, fan, 1dc into next sp. Rep from * to last 2 loops, patt 1 loop, 5ch, 1dc into 3rd of next 5ch, turn.

Row 8: As Row 6.

Row 9: As Row 5.

Row 10: As Row 6.

Row 11: Patt 6 loops, *fan, 1dc into next sp, patt 5 loops.

Rep from * to last loop, 5ch, 1dc into 3rd of next 5ch, turn.

Rows 12–15: Cont patt, completing the 5 diamonds as set over the next 2 RS rows. (End even rows with the 2ch 1tr, as Row 4, and odd rows with 5ch 1dc, as Row 5.)

Row 16: As Row 6.

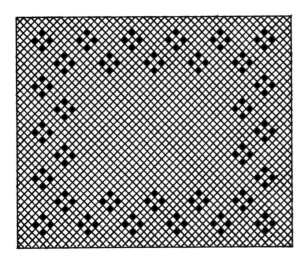

Chart for traycloth

Row 17: Patt 3 loops, fan, 1dc into next sp. Work the (5ch, 1dc) loop patt to last 4 loops, fan, 1dc into next sp, patt to end, turn.
Follow chart above, working fans on every RS row. Include 3 rows of loops after last fan row.
Final row: 4ch, *1dc into next 5ch sp, 3ch.
Rep from * to last loop, 1dc into 3rd of 5ch. Do not turn.

◆

EDGING

Round 1: Start work along short side: 2ch, 2dc into

1st (half) loop sp, *1dc into next (full) loop sp, 2dc into next (half) loop sp. Rep from * to next corner. Long side: 2ch, 2dc into 1st sp, *1dc into next dc stem, 3dc into next sp. Rep from * to 3rd corner. Complete rem sides as above.
Round 2: Ss into 1st 2ch sp, 3ch (tr), 4tr into same sp. Work 1tr into each foll dc and 5tr into each foll 2ch sp, ss into top of 3ch.
Round 3: **(Over 5 corner tr, 3ch, miss next tr, 1dc into next tr) twice, *4ch, miss next 2tr, 1dc into next tr.
Rep from * to next corner, then rep from ** to end. Ss into base of 1st 3ch.
Round 4: 2ss into 1st 3ch sp, 5ch, *1dc into next sp, 5ch.
Rep from * to end, ss into 2nd of 2ss.
Round 5: 1ss into 1st sp, (3ch, 1dc into same sp) twice, 3ch, 1dc into next sp (3 3ch loops made), * 5ch, 1dc into next sp.
Rep from * to end, but around each corner work 2 3ch loops into corner loop and 1 3ch loop each side of same loop (4 3ch loops). At end, complete 1st corner with 3ch loop, ss into ss.
Round 6: 1ss into next sp, 5ch, *1dc into next sp, 5ch. Rep from * to end, ss into ss. Break yarn.
Round 7: With sewing cotton, work 1dc into each st to end. Ss.
Fasten off. Sew in ends.

TABLECLOTH

✳✳✳

This large and beautiful piece is made from repeated motifs, joined together as they are worked, so as to avoid unsightly seams. An edging adds the finishing touch to this delicate, cotton tablecloth.

◆

MATERIALS
280g (10½oz) Coats No 20 Crochet Cotton
Hook 1.25

◆

TENSION
Work to complete one motif to equal
approx 7cm (3in) sq

◆

MEASUREMENTS
Approx 90cm (36in) sq
(20g (1oz) = approx 14 motifs)

◆

METHOD FOR INDIVIDUAL MOTIFS
(See Fig 1)
Make 4ch. Join with ss into circle.
Round 1: 12ch, 1ss into 5th ch from hook (loop), 3ch, (1dtr into 1st circle, 8ch, 1ss into 5th ch from hook, 3ch) 3 times, 1dc into 4th of 1st 12ch. (4sps).
Round 2: (Miss next 3ch, 9tr into next loop, miss next 3ch, 1dc into next dtr) 4 times.
Round 3: 5ch (dtr+1ch), 1dtr into same place as

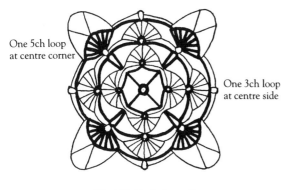

Fig 1 Tablecloth motif

One 5ch loop at centre corner

One 3ch loop at centre side

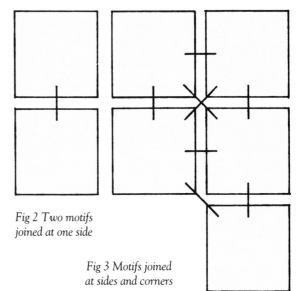

Fig 2 Two motifs joined at one side

Fig 3 Motifs joined at sides and corners

5ch, *5ch, (1dc, 3ch, 1dc) into centre tr of next 9tr, 5ch, (1dtr, 1ch, 1dtr) into next dc.
Rep from * to end, omitting last (1dtr, 1ch, 1dtr) at end of round, ss into 4th of 1st 5ch.

Round 4: *(1dc, 3ch, 1dc) into next 1ch sp, 3ch, 9tr into next 3ch loop, 3ch.
Rep from * to end, ss into 1st 3ch loop.

Round 5: 3ch (tr), 8tr into same loop as 3ch, *6ch, 1dc into centre tr of next 9tr, 6ch, 9tr into next 3ch loop.
Rep from * to end, omitting last 9tr at end of round.

Round 6: (1dc, 3ch, 1dc) into 1st tr of 1st 9tr, *5ch, (1dtr, 5ch, 1dtr) into centre tr of same 9tr, 5ch, (1dc, 3ch, 1dc) into 9th tr of same 9tr, 6ch, (1dc, 3ch, 1dc) into same place as next dc (centre tr), 6ch, (1dc, 3ch, 1dc) into 1st tr of next 9tr.
Rep from * to end, omitting last (1dc, 3ch, 1dc) at end of round. Ss into base of next 3ch.

JOINING MOTIFS

Work 1 motif. Complete 5 rounds of a 2nd motif. Join 2nd motif to 1st motif in one place – at centre of 4th side of Rnd 6 (see Fig 2).
Motifs are joined on Rnd 6 by breaking into the 3ch loop at centre side or 5ch loop at centre corner (see Fig 3, and Fig 4 overleaf), so instead of working (1dc, 3ch for loop, 1dc) at centre of 4th side on 2nd motif, work (1dc into 2nd motif, 1ch, 1dc into a corresponding 3ch loop on 1st motif (inserting hook from beneath), 1ch, 1dc into 2nd motif). Complete round to end. To join together motif corners, instead of working (1dtr, 5ch, 1dtr), work (1dtr, 2ch, 1dc into a diagonally corresponding 5ch loop, 2ch, 1dtr).
Where four corners meet, the first diagonal pair are joined as above; the second diagonal pair are joined as above, but enclose also the first pair with the 1dc (see Fig 3).

Continue to join motifs at sides and/or corners as and where necessary until 13 × 13 motifs square, or required size (see Fig 4, page 62).

EDGING

Round 1: With RS facing, and approx halfway between two tablecloth corners, join yarn to a 3ch loop at centre-side of one motif.
Work 11ch, 1dc into next 5ch corner sp, 3ch, *1dc into next 5ch corner sp on foll motif, 11ch, 1dc into next centre-side loop, 11ch, 1dc into next 5ch corner sp, 3ch. Rep from * to next tablecloth corner.
Form a corner loop by working another dc into same corner sp, 11ch, 1dc into next centre-side loop.
Cont the patt until end of round. End with 1dc into 1st centre-side loop.

Round 2: 2ch, *(1dc, 2ch) 6 times into next 11ch sp, (1tr, 2ch) 6 times into next 3ch sp, (1dc, 2ch) 6 times into next 11ch sp.
Rep from * to end, 1dc into 1st loop.

Round 3: 2ch, (1dc into next loop, 2ch) 5 times, * miss next 2ch. Between trs, (1dc into next 2ch sp, 2ch) 5 times (=4 loops), miss next 2ch, (1dc into next 2ch sp, 2ch) 11 times.
Rep from * to end, working (1dc, 2ch) only 6 times at end of round. 1dc into 1st loop.

Round 4: Cont with the (2ch, 1dc) patt and, as before, work 2ch over 2ch at each side of tr gps (= 3 loops between 2 missed 2ch).
End round with ss.

Fig 4 *An attractive star pattern is revealed when corners are joined*

CAKE FRILL

✳

Add the finishing touch to a cake for that special occasion with this pretty frill, quickly and easily worked in cotton with ribbon trims.

◆

MATERIALS
50g (2oz) DMC Cebelia No 10 Crochet Cotton
Hook 1.75
4.75m × 3mm (5yd × ⅛in) satin ribbon
(6 x length of frill plus 24cm (9½in)
extra for turning under)
Matching sewing thread
Sewing needle
Wool needle

Narrow ribbon oddments for bows (or packet
of 10 small bows)

◆

TENSION
34tr = 10cm (4in) across

◆

MEASUREMENTS
Approx 73 × 8cm (28½ × 3in)

◆

METHOD
Make 215ch.
Row 1: 1tr into 4th ch from hook, 1tr into each foll ch to end, turn.
Row 2: 3ch (1st st), 1tr into each foll sp between trs to end, 1tr into end st, turn.

Row 3: 3ch (1st st), miss 1st sp, 1tr into each foll sp to last sp, miss sp, work 1tr into end st, turn.

Rows 4–6: Rep last 2 rows once more, then Row 2 again.

Row 7: (Frill) *15ch, 1dc into next st. Rep from * to 1cm from end. Break yarn and fasten off.

With same side (RS) facing, join yarn 1cm (½in) from end of base ch and rep last row to match opp side.

Thread ribbon onto wool needle and weave between trs. Leave 2cm (¾in) extra at each end of ribbons. Cut and secure ends onto WS.

Space 10 bows evenly along cake frill and stitch centres.

TEA COSY

✳✳

Worked mainly in dc and tr, this tea cosy has the advantage of a lining to help keep a teapot really hot. All around are twelve little cups hanging on hooks, with their saucers standing on a rack beneath. Some simple embroidery decorates the top, and a solid handle completes the picture. You could crochet the cosy in colours to complement a favourite tea set.

•

MATERIALS

Patons Diploma Gold DK Yarn 100g (3¾oz) each
of main colour (MC) and contrasting colour (CC)
50g (2oz) 3rd colour for cups and saucers
4th colour oddments for rims
Hook 4.50 for cosy; 3.50 for crockery
Piece of broom handle or cotton reel for cosy handle
Wool needle

•

TENSION

15sts and 14 rounds (over long and short
st patt) = 10cm (4in)

•

MEASUREMENTS

Height excluding handle = 19cm (7½in)
Inner and outer circumferences = 52cm (20in)
and 54cm (21in)

•

METHOD

With CC yarn and 4.50 hook, make 87ch. Join into untwisted circle with ss.

Round 1: 1ch (1st dc), 1dc into each foll ch to end, ss into 1st dc. (87sts).

Rounds 2–4: 1ch (1st dc), 1dc into each foll st to end, ss into 1st dc.

Round 5: Join MC with 2ch (1st dc), 1dc into back top loop only of each foll st to end (hemline), ss into top of 2ch.

Cont with MC.

Round 6: 1ch (1st dc), *1tr into next st, 1dc into foll st.

Rep from * to end, 1tr into 1st dc.

Rounds 7–23: Cont by working 1dc into each tr, and 1tr into each dc (long and short st), without ss at end of each round, for 17 more rounds. End with 1dc.

Change to CC. Work 1ss into next st.

Round 24: 1ch (1st dc), dc to end, dec 3sts evenly over round, ss into 1st dc.

Round 25: 1ch (1st dc), 1dc into each foll st to end, ss into 1st dc.

Round 26: 1ch (1st dc), 1dc into next st, 5ch (cup loop), *1dc into each of next 7sts, 5ch.

Rep from * to last 5sts, 5dc to end, ss into 1st dc. (12 loops).

Round 27: 1ch (1st dc). Bringing loops forward to RS, work 1dc into next dc and each foll dc to end. Change to MC, ss into 1st dc. (84sts).

Round 28: 1ch (1st dc), 1tr into next st, *1dc into next st, 1tr into foll st.

Rep from * to end, ss into 1st dc.

Round 29: 3ch (1st tr), 1dc into next st, *1tr into next st, 1dc into foll st.

Rep from * to end.

Change to CC, ss into top of 3ch.

Round 30: 1ch (1st dc), dc to end, dec 7sts evenly over round, ss into 1st dc. (continued on page 66)

Cake Frill (page 62); Napkin Rings (page 67);
Tea Cosy (page 63)

Rounds 31–33: Rep last round 3 times more, varying positions of decs. Change to MC for ss of final round.

Rounds 34–35: Rep Rnds 28 and 29 once more.

Round 36: (CC)1ch (1st dc), dc to end, dec 11sts evenly over round, ss into 1st dc.

Round 37: As last round. Change to MC for ss of round.

Rounds 38–40: Rep Rnds 28 and 29 once, then Rnd 28 again. (34sts).

Break off MC and cont in CC, without ss, to end (see below).

◆

LINING

Rounds 41–43: Dc to end. Cont in htr throughout.

Rounds 44–47: Inc 10sts evenly over each round. (74sts).

Round 48: Htr to end.

Round 49: Inc 8sts over round.

Rounds 50 and 51: Htr to end.

Round 52: Inc 3sts over round.

Cont on these sts until lining, when folded through to inside, reaches approx 1cm (½in) from hemline. End with 2dc, 1ss.

Break yarn and fasten off. Darn in all ends except last end, to allow for any adjustment which may be needed.

Smooth out both fabrics. Insert pins from RS to hold lining evenly in position. Fold first few rounds (CC) of cosy base to inside, allowing hemline to sit neatly at edge.

Enclose base of lining inside, adjusting lining length if necessary, and stitch hem.

◆

SAUCER RACK

(4.50 hook, CC yarn)

Make 90ch. Join with ss into circle. (Check for fit around widest part of cosy and if necessary adjust no of ch, which must be divisible by 3.)

Round 1: 1ch (1st dc), 1dc into each foll ch to end, ss into 1st dc.

Round 2: 4ch (1st htr + 2ch), miss next 2sts, *1htr into next st, 2ch, miss next 2sts.

Rep from * to end, ss into 2nd of 4ch.

Round 3: 4dc into each 2ch sp to end, ss into 1st dc. Fasten off.

◆

SAUCER

(3.50 hook, 3rd col yarn. Make 12)

Wind yarn once around little finger, slip off, hold-

Begin saucer with a loop to avoid a centre hole

ing circle. Insert hook through centre and draw yarn through to front (see above):

Round 1: Make 1ch, 6dc into circle. Pull free end to close circle, ss into 1st dc. (6sts).

Round 2: 1ch (1st dc), 1dc into same place as 1ch, 2dc into each foll dc to end, ss into 1st dc. (12sts).

Round 3: 1ch (1st dc), 1dc into next st, 2dc into foll st, (1dc into each of next 2sts, 2dc into foll st) 3 times, ss into 1st dc.

Round 4: 1ch (1st dc), 1dc into each of next 2sts, 2dc into next st, (1dc into each of next 3sts, 2dc into foll st) 3 times, ss into 1st dc.

Round 5: 1ch (1st dc), 2dc into next st, (1dc into each of next 4sts, 2dc into next st) 3 times, work 3dc to end, ss into 1st dc. Break off yarn.

Round 6: With 4th col yarn, work 1 round of ss on WS, for rim. Fasten off.

Backstitch a circle with wool needle between 1st two rounds.

◆

CUP

(3.50 hook, 3rd col yarn. Make 12)

Make 3ch. Join with ss into circle.

Round 1: 1ch, 6dc into circle, ss into 1st dc. (6sts).

Round 2: 1ch (1st dc). Working into back top loops of dc for this round only, 1dc into next st, 2dc into next st, 1dc into each of next 2sts, 2dc into next st, ss into 1st dc.

Round 3: 1ch (1st dc), (2dc into next st, 1dc into foll st) 3 times, 2dc into last st, ss into 1st dc.

Round 4: 1ch (1st dc), 1dc into each of next 2sts, (2dc into next st, 1dc into each of next 3sts) twice, 2dc into last st, ss into 1st dc.

Round 5: 1ch (1st dc), 1dc into each of next 4sts, 2dc into next st, 1dc into each of next 6sts, 2dc into next st, 2dc to end, ss into 1st dc. (17sts).

Rounds 6 and 7: 1ch (1st dc), dc to end, ss into 1st dc.

Work 9ch for handle, 1ss into single loop at back of 2nd ch from hook, and each of next 7ch.

Break off 3rd col yarn.

Round 8: (Rim) With 4th col yarn, make 1ch, 1dc into each st of Rnd 7, ss into 1st dc. Break yarn and fasten off.

◆

HANDLE

(4.50 hook, CC yarn)
Make a cover for cotton reel as follows:
Make 3ch. Join with ss into circle.
Round 1: 3ch (1st tr), 11tr into circle, ss into top of 3ch.
Round 2: 1ch (1st dc), 2dc into next st, *1dc into next st, 2dc into foll st.
Rep from * to end, ss into 1st dc. Without inc, work dc rounds to length of reel using a different colour (of the 4 colours used) for each round.
Break off yarns and sew in ends.
Make a second circle for top of reel and stitch all tog around reel. Gather cosy top around handle and stitch securely. With MC and wool needle, work 4

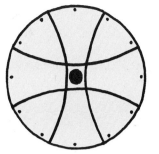

Bird's-eye view of the cosy, with handle at centre, showing position for four arcs of stitching

arcs of stem stitch across top of cosy, using doubled yarn (see above).
Pin saucers evenly around cosy at 2.5cm (1in) from cosy base. Stitch close to centres.
Work a round of backstitch attaching rack base to cosy, so that saucer bases show through holes. Work another round, near to top of rack, catching rims of saucers twice. Thread cup handles through loops and stitch.

NAPKIN RINGS

✳✳

Once you have mastered the knack of making these simple 'popcorn' motifs, you will find it quick and easy to form them into pretty napkin rings. Decorated with satin ribbon, they turn teatime into party time!

◆

MATERIALS

50g (2oz) Twilleys Secco No 3 Cotton (4 ply)
(enough for 6 napkin rings)
Hook 3.50
Double-faced satin ribbon
50 × 0.75cm (20 × ¼in)
Wool needle

◆

POPCORN MOTIF

Make 6ch. Join with ss into circle. 3ch (tr), 4tr into circle.
To make a popcorn, remove hook from last (5th) tr, insert hook from front into top of 1st of the 5tr, behind 2nd, 3rd and 4th tr, catch loop of 5th tr onto hook, and draw through. Keep fairly tight.
Work 3ch, (5tr into circle, make a popcorn with these 5tr, 3ch) 5 times. Ss into closing st behind 1st popcorn. Break yarn and fasten off.
Make another popcorn motif, but instead of working the final 3ch, make 1ch, ss into any 3ch loop of prev motif, make another 1ch, then ss into closing st behind 1st popcorn.
Join on 2 more motifs so that there are 4 motifs in a straight line.
To form a ring, join a 5th motif to last and 1st motifs by interrupting both 3rd and final 3ch loop with the 1ch, 1ss, 1ch as before.
Using wool needle, thread a line of ribbon over joined ch loops, and behind each motif (see below). Pull ribbon up very slightly through centre holes, and make a small stitch underneath ribbon and across hole to secure. Tie ends in a small bow.

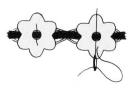

Thread ribbon over loop joins and behind each motif

CHAPTER FIVE

The Bedroom

Bedspread (page 70); Hot Water Bottle Cover (page 71);
Filet Bedlinen Edgings (page 72)

BEDSPREAD

✳ ✳ ✳

Motifs, made up of ovals within long hexagons, are crocheted together to create a pretty fabric, which is then adorned with decorative fringing around the edge.

◆

MATERIALS

4 ply Cotton:
2350g (83oz) for standard single size
3000g (106oz) for standard double size
Hook 3.50

◆

TENSION

1st 3 rounds = 7.75 × 6.25cm (3 × 2½in)

◆

MOTIF

Approx 18 × 16cm (7 × 6in)
50g (2oz) = approx 4 motifs
40m (45yd) = 1 motif
Single bedspread 175 motifs
Double bedspread 229 motifs

◆

MEASUREMENTS

(excluding fringe)
264 × 180cm (104 × 70in) single size
264 × 232cm (104 × 90in) double size

◆

OVAL/HEXAGON MOTIF

Make 6ch. Join with ss into circle.
Round 1: 3ch (1st tr). Into circle, work 5tr, 3dtr, 6tr, 3dtr. Ss into top of 3ch.
Round 2: 1ss between 1st 2tr, 2ch (1st htr), 1htr into 2nd ch from hook, (1htr between next 2 sts. Work 1htr into last sp made by inserting hook, from front, around stem of last htr made = hp). Cont in this way by working 1hp into each foll sp between sts to end, ss into top of 2ch. (18htr pairs).
Round 3: (1ss into next st, 1ss into 1st sp = 2ss), 2ch (1st htr), 1htr into 2nd ch from hook, 1hp into each of next 5sps (of rem 17sps between hps), 2hp (inc) into next sp, 1hp into each of next 8sps, 2hp into next sp, 1hp into each of next 2sps, ss into top of 2ch. (20hp).
Round 4: 2ss, 2ch (1st htr), 1htr into 2nd ch from

hook, 1hp into each of next 4sps, 2hp into next sp, 1hp into each of next 9sps, 2hp into next sp, 1hp into each of next 4sps, ss into top of 2ch. (22hp). Pull to shape.
Round 5: 2ss, 2ch (1st htr), (1dc, 1htr) into 2nd ch from hook, (1htr into next sp. Work both 1dc and 1htr into last sp made – inserting hook, from front, around stem of last htr made = dhp). 1dhp into each of next 4sps, 2dhp into each of next 2sps, 1dhp into each of next 9sps, 2dhp into each of next 2sps, 1dhp into each of next 3sps, ss into 1st dc. (26dhp). Cont to pull gently into shape.
Round 6: 2ss, 2ch (1st htr), (1dc, 2htr) into 2nd ch from hook (1htr into next sp – under 3 strands. Work 1dc and 2htr into last sp made, around stem of last htr made = dhhp), 1dhhp into each foll sp to end, ss into top of 2ch. (26dhhp).
Round 7: (4ch, 1dc tightly into next sp) to end. (26 loops).
Round 8: 1ss into 1st 4ch sp, 3ch (1st tr), 1htr into 2nd ch from hook, 3ch.
Into same 4ch sp, work (1tr, 1htr around stem of last tr = ht), 1ch, **(1ht, 1ch) into next sp, (1hp, 1ch) into each of next 2sps, (1ht, 1ch) into next sp, (1ht, 3ch, 1ht, 1ch) into next sp, (1hp, 1ch) into each of next 2sps, (1ht, 3ch, 1ht, 1ch) into next sp, (1ht, 1ch) into next sp, (1hp, 1ch) into each of next 2sps, (1ht, 1ch) into next sp, *(1ht, 3ch, 1ht, 1ch) into next sp.
Rep from ** to * once more, ss into top of 1st 3ch.
Round 9: 2ss, 3ch (1st tr), 1htr into 2nd ch from hook, 3ch, 1ht into same sp, 1ch.
Cont to end with (1ht, 1ch) into each 1ch sp, and (1ht, 3ch, 1ht, 1ch) into each 3ch sp. Ss into top of 1st 3ch.

◆

LAYOUT AND JOINING MOTIFS

The 2 shorter sides of motifs are laid parallel with head and toe ends of bed. Beg and ending with a 13 motif line, the bedspread is made with alternate lines of 13 and 14 motifs running from head to toe, the 14 motif lines being ½ motif longer each end. For a single beadspread, make 13 of these lines. For a double size, make 17 lines.
Motifs are crocheted together on RS by working

FILET BEDLINEN EDGINGS

❋❋

 Transform even the plainest sheets and pillowcases – for yourself or your guests – with these attractive filet crochet edgings.

◆

FILET

Sp = 1tr,2ch,1tr. Change the 2ch to 2tr to form a block of 4tr. (Last st of sq counts as 1st st of next sq.) For further instructions on filet crochet, see p11.

◆

MATERIALS

Sheet
100g (3¾oz) DMC Cebelia No 20 Crochet Cotton
Hook 1.50
Pillowcase
20g (1oz) DMC Cebelia No 20 Crochet Cotton
Hook 1.50
Approx 0.5m (20in) narrow double-faced satin
ribbon

Matching sewing threads
Sewing needle

◆

TENSION/MEASUREMENTS

Sheet
(Without ch and picot edging)
Width = 10 and 13.5cm (4 and 5½in) at narrowest
and widest points
12-row patt = 6½cm (2½in)

Pillowcase
(With ch edging)
Width = 5.5cm (2in)
at widest point
6-row patt =3cm (1¼in)

◆

METHOD FOR SHEET

Make 51ch.
Row 1: 1tr into 4th ch from hook, 1tr into each of

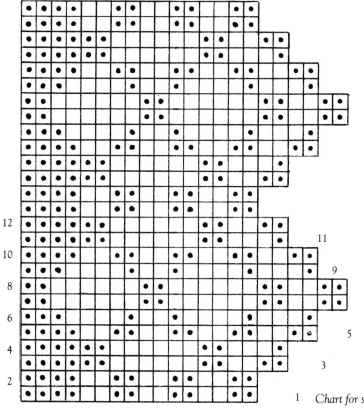

1   *Chart for sheet edging*

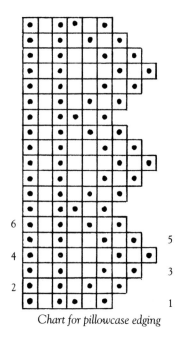

Chart for pillowcase edging

next 5ch, *(2ch, miss next 2ch, 1tr into next ch) twice, 1tr into each of next 6ch.
Rep from * twice more. Work 1tr into each of next 6ch, turn.
Follow chart (see below left) from Row 2, shaping as shown. Patt repeats after Row 12.

Edging: Around pointed edge, work a picot of (1dc,3ch,1dc) into each inner and outer corner. Link the picots with 5ch and 6ch respectively along horizontal (tr sides) and vertical 'steps' (tr tops). Across tips only, work 6ch between picots (see below).
Hand- or machine-stitch straight side of edging to edge of sheet.

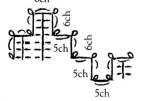

Sheet edging showing picots at inner and outer corners, with linking chains

METHOD FOR PILLOWCASE

Make 21ch.
Row 1: 1tr into 4th ch from hook, 1tr into each of next 2ch, 2ch, miss next 2ch, 1tr into each of next 7ch, 2ch, miss next 2ch, 1tr into each of next 4ch, turn.
Follow chart (see page 72, right) from Row 2, shaping as shown. Patt repeats after Row 6.

Edging: Join yarn to outer corner at start of 1st row, and work around points as follows:
(3ch,1dc) into each of next 3 outer corners, 3ch across tip, 1dc into next corner (same block), (3ch,1dc) into each of next 2 corners, 3ch across centre, 1dc into next outer corner. Continue similarly to end.
Slot ribbon through sps at one block in from straight edge. Hem ends on WS of edging.
Hand-stitch straight side of edging to open edge of pillowcase, through one thickness of pocketed fabric. Allow point tips to rest fairly close to fold.

DUCHESSE SET

٭

This deceptively simple network of chains is quickly worked into useful and attractive mats that lend the classic finishing touch to a dressing table.

◆

MATERIALS

40g (1¾oz) Coats Crochet Cotton No 10
Hook 1.75

◆

MEASUREMENTS

Small mat 17 × 15cm (6½ ×6in)
Large mat 28 × 24cm (11 × 9½in)

◆

METHOD

For small mat (make two), make 66ch; for large mat, make 116ch (see page 74).
Row 1: 1dc into 11th ch from hook, make 11ch, 1dc into same base ch as last dc, 5ch, miss next 4 base ch, 1dc into next ch, *5ch, miss next 4 base ch, (1dc,11ch,1dc) into next ch, 5ch, miss next 4 base ch, 1dc into next ch. Rep from * to end, turn.
Row 2: 7ch, miss 1st 5ch loop, 1dc into centre (6th) ch st of next 11ch loop, 6ch, *1dc into dc between next 2 5ch loops, 6ch, miss next 5ch, 1dc into centre ch st of next 11ch loop, 6ch.
Rep from * to end, miss remainder of 11ch loop and next 5ch, 1dc into next ch st, turn.
Row 3: 10ch, 1dc into dc at tip of 1st 11ch loop, *9ch, 1dc into dc at tip of next 11ch loop.
Rep from * ending row with 4ch, 1ttr into end ch st of next 7ch, turn.
Row 4: 6ch, (1dc,11ch,1dc) into next dc, 5ch, *1dc into centre ch st of next 9ch, 5ch, (1dc,11ch, 1dc) into next dc, 5ch.
Rep from * to end, miss next 4ch, 1dc into next ch st, turn.
Small mat: Rep Rows 2–4, 5 times more.
Large mat: Rep Rows 2–4, 10 times more.
Both mats: Rep Rows 2 and 3, once more.

Small mat

Large mat

*Interlaced chains
produce a reversible fabric*

Final row: 5ch, 1dc into next dc, 5ch, *1dc into centre ch st of next 9ch, 5ch, 1dc into next dc, 5ch. Rep from * to end, miss next 4ch, 1dc into next ch st, turn.

◆

BORDER

1st side: 5ch, 1dc into 1st 5ch sp, *5ch, 1dc into next 5ch sp. Rep from * to end, 5ch, 1dc into top of ttr. Do not turn.

2nd side: 5ch, 1dc into centre of 1st triangle sp (around ttr stem), *8ch, 1dc into identical triangle sp of next 3-row pattern. Rep from * to end, 5ch, 1dc into corner st. Complete rem sides to match.

TABLE-TOP OR CHEST COVER

✳✳

More-or-less filet crochet, the openwork rows of this cover create very gentle scallops along each side.

◆

MATERIALS

1 ball = approx 50–60g (2–2½oz)
Twilleys Southern Comfort Crochet Cotton
(3 ply: ball = 363/411m [400/450yd])
Hook 2.50
Sewing thread and needle
Piece of stiff card, 11cm (4in) sq

◆

TENSION

29tr and 13 rows = 10cm (4in) sq

◆

MEASUREMENTS

50 × 36cm (19½ × 14in)

◆

METHOD

Make 98ch (or any no divisible by 10 minus 2), not too tightly.

Row 1: 1tr into 4th ch from hook, 1tr into each foll ch to end, turn.

Row 2: 3ch (1st st), 1tr into next st, 2ch, miss next 2sts, *1tr into each of next 8sts, 2ch, miss next 2sts. Rep from * to last 2sts, 2tr, turn.

Row 3: 3ch (1st st), 1tr into next st, 2ch, miss next 2ch, *1tr into each of next 8sts, 2ch, miss next 2ch. Rep from * to last 2sts, 2tr, turn.

Rows 4–9: Rep last row, 6 times more.

Row 10: 3ch (1st st), 1tr into next st, 2ch, miss next 2ch, *1tr into each of next 3sts, 2ch, miss next 2sts, 1tr into each of next 3sts, 2ch, miss next 2ch. Rep from * to last 2sts, 2tr, turn.

Row 11: 3ch (1st st), 1tr into next st, 2ch, miss next 2ch, *1tr into next st, 2ch, miss next 2sts, 2tr into next sp, 2ch, miss next 2sts, 1tr into next st, 2ch, miss next 2ch. Rep from * to last 2sts, 2tr, turn.

Row 12: 3ch (1st st), 1tr into next st, 2ch, miss next 2ch, *1tr into next st, 2tr into next sp, 2ch, miss next 2sts, 2tr into next sp, 1tr into next st, 2ch, miss next 2ch. Rep from * to last 2sts, 2tr, turn.

Row 13: 3ch (1st st), 1tr into next st, 2ch, miss next 2ch, *1tr into each of next 3sts, 2tr into next sp, 1tr into each of next 3sts, 2ch, miss next 2ch. Rep from * to last 2sts, 2tr, turn. Rep Rows 3–13, 5 times more (or to desired length, less approx 5.5cm (2in)). Rep Row 3, 7 times more.

Final row: 3ch (1st st), 1tr into next st, 2tr into next sp, *1tr into each of next 8sts, 2tr into next sp. Rep from * to last 2sts, 2tr.

Break yarn and fasten off.

CORNERS

Working along base row towards slip-knot at 1st corner, rejoin yarn at sp between 10th and 11th tr from same corner, 1ch, 1dc into sp between 9th and 10th tr, 3ch, 1dc into next sp, (4ch, 1dc) into each of next 2sps, (5ch, 1dc) into each of next 3sps, (6ch, 1dc) into each of next 2sps, 8ch, 1dc again into final sp – do not turn.

Cont around corner along side: 7ch, 1dc into sp between 2tr at end of 2nd row, 6ch, 1dc into same sp, (5ch, 1dc) into each of next 2sps, 4ch, 1dc into next sp, 3ch, 1dc into same sp, 3ch, 1dc into next sp, 2ch, 1dc into same sp, 2ch, 1dc into each of next 2sps. (Ending at 8th row.)

Complete diagonally opp corner to match. Match rem corners, starting at 8th rows (see below).

TASSEL TOP

(Make 4)

Make 4ch. Join with ss into circle.

Round 1: Work 8dc into circle.

Rounds 2–5: Dc to end. (8sts).

Round 6: 1ss into next st, *1ch, 1ss into next st. Rep from * to end. Break yarn and fasten off, leaving a 20cm (8in) end for stitching.

To complete a tassel, wind some yarn 30 times around the piece of card. Remove, and fit loop ends into tassel top opening. Gather around edge, and stitch to secure. Cut open rem loops. Stitch tassels to 8ch loops at corners of cover.

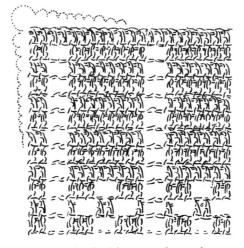

Pattern sketch of the cover, showing loops increasing in size towards one corner

SMALL CUSHION

✳ ✳

A small variation of normal dc produces the firm fabric which makes up most of this cosy cushion. Two lengths of pointed edging, one in each colour, are made separately, joined along the pointed side and lightly padded. The 'tinklebell' tops are shaped by winding invisible thread just below the tip of each point. Decorated cords complete the cushion.

♦

MATERIALS

200g (7¼oz) main colour (MC);
100g (3¾oz) contrasting colour (CC)
of Jaeger Cotton DK Yarn
Hooks 4.00, 3.50 and 3.00
Invisible sewing thread
Wool and sewing needles
Small amount of wadding for pendant and border
Cushion pad

♦

TENSION

19sts and 21 rows = 10cm (4in) sq

♦

MEASUREMENTS

33 × 36cm (13 × 14in) (excluding border)

♦

METHOD

(Two pieces alike)
With MC and 4.00 hook, make 51ch.
Row 1: (RS) 1dc into 2nd ch from hook, 1dc into each foll ch to end, turn (50sts).
Row 2: 2ch (1st st), 1dc into 1st st to make an increased st, 1dc into each of next 2sts, *1dc into back top loop of next st, 1dc into front top loop of foll st.

ABOVE: Duchesse Set (page 73)

RIGHT: Small Cushion (this page); Table Top or Chest Cover (page 74)

Rep from * to last 3sts, (both loops) 1dc into next st, 2dc into next st, 1dc into final st, turn.

Cont to work the few sts at each end in normal dc.

Row 3: 2ch (1st st), 1dc into 1st st (inc), 1dc into each of next 2sts, *1dc into front top loop of next st, 1dc into back top loop of foll st.

Rep from * to last 3sts, 1dc into next st, 2dc into next st, 1dc into final st, turn.

Rows 4–7: Rep last 2 rows twice more (62sts).

Row 8: 1ch (1st st), 1dc into each of next 2sts, *1dc into back top loop of next st, 1dc into front top loop of foll st. Rep from * to last 3sts, 3dc, turn.

Rep last row until work measures approx 26cm (10¼in). End with WS row.

Decrease edges as follows:

Row 1:(RS) 2ch (1st st), dc2tog, 1dc into next dc, *1dc into front top loop of next st, 1dc into back top loop of foll st.

Rep from * to last 4sts, 1dc into next st, dc2tog, 1dc into final dc, turn.

Row 2: 2ch (1st st), dc2tog, 1dc into next st, *1dc into back top loop of next st, 1dc into front top loop of foll st.

Rep from * to last 4sts, 1dc into next st, dc2tog, 1dc into final st, turn.

Rep last 2 rows until 50 sts remain.

◆

INNER BORDER

Round 1: Working in normal dc, join CC yarn and make 2ch (1st st), 1dc into 1st st (inc), *work 48dc to last st, 2dc into next st.

Do not turn. Work along decreased edge.

5dc to next point, 2dc into next st, 36dc evenly along (straight) side, 2dc into next point, 5dc along increased edge, 2dc into start of base ch.

Cont to end of round, matching first 2 sides. Omit the final 2dc. End with ss into top of 1st 2ch.

Round 2: 1ch (1st st), dc to end, change colour, ss into 1st st.

Round 3: (MC) As Rnd 2 but inc 1 st at each of the 8 'corners', change colour, ss into 1st st.

Round 4: (CC) As Rnd 2 (without colour change).

Round 5: (CC) As Rnd 3.

Break yarn and fasten off.

◆

POINTED BORDER

(Make one of each colour)

With same hook, make 3ch.

Row 1: 1dc into 2nd ch from hook, 1dc into next ch, turn.

Row 2: 1ch (1st st), 1dc into next st, turn.

Row 3: 3ch, 1dc into 2nd ch from hook, 1dc into next ch, 2dc to end, turn.

Row 4: 1ch (1st st), 3dc to end, turn.

Row 5: 3ch, 1dc into 2nd ch from hook, 1dc into next ch, 4dc to end, turn.

Row 6: 1ch (1st st), 5dc to end, turn.

Row 7: 3ch, 1dc into 2nd ch from hook, 1dc into next ch, 6dc to end, turn.

Rows 8 and 9: 1ch (1st st), 1dc into each of next 5sts, turn.

Rows 10 and 11: 1ch (1st st), 1dc into each of next 3sts, turn.

Rows 12 and 13: 1ch (1st st), 1dc into next st, turn.

Rep Rows 2-13 until 17 complete points have been worked. Break yarn and fasten off.

Place the 2 pointed borders together, with one slip-knot on lhs and other on rhs.

Leave each straight edge unworked. With either colour yarn and same hook, join the stepped edges by picking up (both together) single loops from one colour (inc rows) and two loops from second colour (dec rows). Join at rhs, work 2dc up each of first 3 step sides, 1ss into 1st st of 4th step side, 3dc into 2nd st of same step.

*Omit the tip, and work down 2nd side: 3dc into 1st st of same top step, 1ss into 2nd st of same step, 2dc down each of 2nd and 3rd step sides, dc2tog (working into between-st at centre and 1st st of next 1st step). 1dc into 2nd st of 1st step, 2dc up next step, 1ss into 1st st of next step, 3dc into 2nd st of same step (see below).

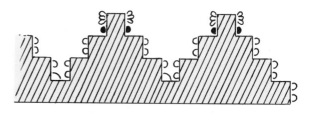

Stitch placement for the pointed border

Rep from * to start of 2nd side of 17th point, 3dc into 1st st, 1ss into 2nd st of top step, 2dc down each of next 3 steps. Break yarn and fasten off.

Using invisible thread, wind tightly around 2ss 'neck' at top of each point, making approx 0.75cm (⅓in) width (see page 79, top).

Sew ends to inside.

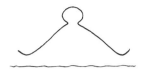

Completed shape after winding invisible thread around tip

Pad each point with triangle of 0.5 to 1cm (¼ to ½in) thick wadding. Oversew loosely with either colour DK yarn all along base edge, to close. Tack straight edge of border with points outwards to WS of one cushion piece, 1cm (½in) from cushion edge, around one long and two shorter sides, starting with 9th point at centre of long side (see below).

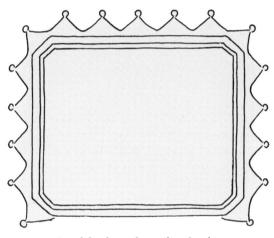

Attach border to three sides of cushion

With WS together, stitch through both cushion pieces and pointed border close to edge.

◆

PENDANT

(Make 2)
First, make a twisted cord with 3 x 85cm (33in) lengths of CC yarn (see Techniques). Leave folded end free. Make a knot approx 3cm (1in) from other end.
Each pendant consists of 4 balls and a ring at each end of an 'acorn' threaded on the cord (see below).

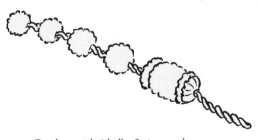

Pendant with 4 balls, 2 rings and acorn

Each ball and space between increases in size. Use MC yarn for pendants.

Ball 1 (3.00 hook)
Wind yarn twice around small finger.
Round 1: Work 5 (clear) dc into circle. Close hole. Stitch end to secure.
Round 2: 2dc into each st to end.
Rounds 3–5: Dc to end.
Break yarn leaving 12cm (4½in) end. Weave end through sts of last round. Stuff ball, place cord knot inside, and pull yarn end to gather top. Secure with a few stitches.

Ball 2 (3.50 hook)
Follow instructions for Ball 1, but only partially close base hole. Thread onto cord, close and stitch base hole, leaving approx 0.5cm (¼in) space between balls. Stuff, gather and secure.

Ball 3 (3.50 hook)
As Ball 2, but work 6dc into circle instead of 5dc. Thread onto cord leaving 1cm (½in) space.

Ball 4 (3.50 hook)
Start as Ball 2, but work 7dc into circle.
Rep Rnds 2, 3 and 4.
Round 5: *dc2tog.
Rep from * to end.
Thread onto cord. Tighten base and secure. Add another dc round. Stuff, gather and secure.

Ring (3.50 hook. Make 2)
Make 8ch. Join with ss into circle.
Round 1: 15dc into circle. Sew in end.
Work 2 more rounds of longer dc into circle, to cover 1st round, with 1ss at end.

Acorn (3.50 hook)
Start as Ball 2, but work 7dc into circle.
Rep Rnd 2. Work 5 dc rounds.
Round 8: *dc2tog.
Rep from * to end.
Thread onto cord with RS of rings touching each end of acorn. Stuff acorn, tighten and secure ends. Stitch final round of rings to acorn.
Stitch folded pendant ends to inside of cushion at each side of opening.
Insert shaped pad. Close opening with oversewing using either colour of DK yarn.

Toilet Roll Cover (page 82); Bathmat (page 82); Filet Guest Towel Edgings (page 83)

MEASUREMENTS

Length, including frill = 127cm (50in)
Width, including edging = 170cm (67in)
edge to edge
Make approx 129 motifs for the frill:
a 20g (1oz) ball of crochet cotton will complete
approx 14 motifs.

MOTIF

Make 23ch, fairly tightly.

Row 1: (Filet) 1tr into 8th ch from hook (2ch+tr+2ch), *2ch, miss next 2ch, 1tr into next ch.
Rep from * to end, turn. (6sqs).

Row 2: 5ch (tr+2ch), miss 1st 2ch, 1tr into next tr, *2ch, miss next 2ch, 1tr into next tr.
Rep from * to end, turn.
Rep last row until 6 × 6 filet sqs.
Do not turn. Work around 4 sides as follows:

Round 1: 1ss into same corner sq, 5ch (dtr+ch). Into same sp work (1dtr,1ch) 3 times. *Along next side, miss next sq, 1dc into next sp, 5ch, 1dc into next sp, 1ch, miss next sq, (1dtr,1ch) 11 times into next corner sp.
Rep from * but into final corner sq work (1dtr,1ch) only 7 times. Ss to 4th of 1st 5ch.

Round 2: 1ss into next 1ch sp, 7ch (dtr+3ch), 1dtr into next 1ch sp, 3ch, 1dtr into next sp, *1ch, (miss sp between 11th of same dtr grp and filet), 1dc into next 5ch sp, 1ch, (miss sp between filet and next dtr), 1dtr into next sp, (3ch, 1dtr) into each of next 9sps.
Rep from * along rem sides but into 1ch sps of final corner work (1dtr,3ch) only 7 times. Ss to 4th of 7ch.

The frill consists of 43 motifs wide × 3 motifs deep although once gathered, the number across may need to be adjusted. With sewing thread join motifs together on WS by stitching over and through the 3 ch sts which link the 3rd to 4th dtr and 7th to 8th dtr of a corner.

CANOPY

1 Cut off a 2.5cm (1in) wide ribbon from one raw edge of fabric and leave to one side.
2 Make a 1cm (½in) wide double hem along each raw edge of main fabric.
3 Fold in half, hems together along one side. Make a 15cm (6in) long cut for an opening at one end of fold (top).

4 Using a length of the ribbon, bind around the opening.
5 Tack a single hem along base.
6 Join halves together at the top by firstly pressing 3cm (1¼in) of fabric along rem selvedge edges onto WS. Fold canopy down centre, WS together, and make one line of stitching across the top through 4 layers (and hems), fairly close to selvedge edges.
7 Make a parallel line of stitching through 2 layers to form a 2–2.5cm (¾–1in) wide channel.

GATHERING FRILL

(See below)

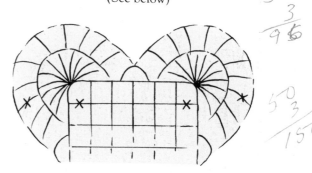

*The four crosses indicate dc positions on one motif
for gathering the frill*

Row 1: Using hook and crochet cotton, work on WS along uppermost row of filet sqs.
Insert hook under base and into sp of 1st corner sq, join yarn and make 2ch. Miss next 4sqs along, 1dc under base and into next corner sp. Work 2ch, 1dc around stem of 3rd dtr (2nd rnd) of same motif, 2ch, 1dc around stem of corresponding dtr of next motif, 2ch, 1dc under base and into next corner sq of 2nd motif.
Continue along frill working (1dc,2ch) 4 times into each motif. Omit final 2ch, and do not work into last dtr. Turn.

Row 2: 3ch(tr), 4tr into 1st 2ch sp, 5tr into each foll 2ch sp to end.
Attach tr row of frill to RS of canopy, completing base hem – allow 2 dtr rounds to protrude over sides on the 3 motifs at each end.

EDGING FOR FRONT OPENING

Make 2 filet ribbons, each the full length of canopy, excluding frill. Work as filet centre of motif, but with only 14ch instead of 23ch (3sqs).
Rejoin yarn to centre sq at one end of a ribbon.

Row 1: Make 1ch. Into next corner sp work (1dtr,1ch) 12 times (ribbon top).

Working along side, miss next sq, 1dc into next sp, 5ch, 1dc into next sp, *1ch, miss next sq, (1dtr,1ch) 6 times into next sp, miss next sq, 1dc into next sp, 5ch, 1dc into next sp.

Rep from * to end of side, leaving last few sqs unworked for tucking under top corner of frill.

Break yarn and fasten off. With RS facing, rejoin to unworked corner sp at opp end of ribbon.

Row 2: Make 3ch, 1dtr into sp between 1st 2dtr, (3ch,1dtr) into each of next 10sps, 1ch, 1dc into next 5ch sp, *1ch, 1dtr into sp between next 2dtr, (3ch, 1dtr) into each of next 4sps, 1ch, 1dc into next 5ch sp. Rep from * to end.

For the 2nd ribbon, leave the same number of sqs unworked as on 1st ribbon, join yarn to next sq and make 5ch, 1dc into next sp, 1ch, miss next sq, *(1dtr;1ch) 6 times into next sp, miss next sq, 1dc into next sp, 5ch, 1dc into next sp, 1ch, miss next sq.

Rep from * to last sq, (1dtr,1ch) 12 times into corner sp, 1dc into centre sq at end of ribbon.

Complete 2nd row from opp end, matching 1st ribbon.

Note the RS of each ribbon.

Pin the 3-sq width of each ribbon to RS of fabric at edges of opening, allowing the 2dtr rows to protrude over sides.

Sew to canopy.

DRESS

❋❋

A sweet little dress, surprisingly straightforward to make, and equally suitable for a girl or a boy.

◆

MATERIALS

100g (3¾oz) Sirdar Snuggly 3 ply Yarn
Hook 3.00
1m (1yd) narrow broderie anglaise trim
2 small buttons
Wool and sewing needles

◆

TENSION

23tr and 17 rows = 10cm (4in) sq
Over loop patt, 10dc+9 loops and
26 rows = 10cm (4in) sq

◆

MEASUREMENTS

Length = 32cm (12½in)
Bodice width = 18cm (7in)
Skirt width = 34cm (13in)
Sleeve length = 5cm (2in)

◆

SKIRT

Beg at skirt top, make 104ch.

Row 1: 1dc into 6th ch from hook, *3ch, miss next ch, 1dc into next ch. Rep from * to end, turn.

Row 2: 3ch, 1dc into 1st loop, (3ch, 1dc) into each of next 2 loops, *inc 1 loop by working 2ch, 1dc into same loop as last dc, (3ch,1dc) into each of next 3 loops.

Rep from * working into only 2 loops at end, turn.

Row 3: 3ch, 1dc into 1st loop, *3ch, 1dc into next loop. Rep from * to end, turn.

Rep last row 15 times more. Omit (3ch,1dc) into last loop of final row (for underlay).

Cont loop patt (with the one less loop) until 23cm (9in) from base ch.

Break yarn and fasten off.

◆

FRONT BODICE

Row 1: Working over centre 20 loops of skirt top, (underlay on lhs), join yarn and make 2ch into 1st of 20 loops (1st st), 1dc into same loop, 2dc into each of next 19 loops, (mark as RS), turn.

Row 2: 3ch (1st st), tr2tog (over next 2dc), 1tr into each foll st to last 3sts, tr2tog, 1tr into last st, turn (38sts).

Row 3: 1ch (1st st), 1dc into each foll st to end, turn.

Row 4: 3ch (1st st), 1tr into each foll st to end, turn.

Rows 5–11: Rep Rows 3 and 4, 3 times more, and Row 3 again.

Matineé Coat (page 94)

RIGHT NECK

Row 1: 3ch (1st st), 2tr into next st, 1tr into each of next 6sts, tr2tog, 1tr into next st. (Mark 17th dc from last tr made, for beg of left neck). Turn.
Rows 2 and 3: 1ch (1st st), work 10dc to end, turn. Break yarn and fasten off.

LEFT NECK

Row 1: With WS facing, rejoin yarn to marked st. Work 3ch (1st st), tr2tog, 1tr into each of next 6sts, 2tr into next st, 1tr into last st, turn.
Rows 2 and 3: 1ch (1st st), work 10dc to end, turn. Break yarn and fasten off.

RIGHT BACK BODICE

Row 1: With RS facing, join yarn to 5th loop (skirt top) from left edge of front bodice. Make 2ch (1st st), 1dc into same loop, 2dc into each of next 10 loops, turn.
Row 2: 3ch (1st st), 1tr into each foll st to last 3sts, tr2tog, 1tr into last st, turn.
Row 3: 1ch (1st st), 1dc into each foll st to end, turn.
Row 4: 3ch (1st st), 1tr into each foll st to end, turn.
Rows 5–11: Rep Rows 3 and 4, 3 times more, and Row 3 again.

Row 12: 3ch (1st st), 1tr into each foll st to last 2sts, 2tr into next st, 1tr into last st, turn.
Row 13: As Row 3. Break yarn and fasten off.
Row 14: Turn to WS. Working towards armhole, rejoin yarn to 11th dc from armhole edge, and rep Row 3 once more. Break yarn and fasten off.

LEFT BACK BODICE

Row 1: With RS facing, join yarn to unworked end loop of skirt top. Make 2ch (1st st), 1dc into same loop, 2dc into each of next 10 loops, turn.
Row 2: 3ch (1st st), tr2tog, 1tr into each foll st to end, turn.
Row 3: 1ch (1st st), 1dc into each foll st to end, turn.
Row 4: 3ch (1st st), 1tr into each foll st to end, turn.
Rows 5–11: Rep Rows 3 and 4, 3 times more, and Row 3 again.
Row 12: 3ch (1st st), 2tr into next st, 1tr into each foll st to end, turn.
Row 13: As Row 3.
Row 14: 1ch (1st st), 1dc into each of next 10sts. Break yarn and fasten off.
Join shoulders by oversewing on WS.

RIGHT SLEEVE

(Work around dc and tr sts of armhole.)

Row 1: With RS facing, join yarn (near underarm) to 1st dc row of right back bodice, *(3ch, miss next tr row, 1dc into end of next dc row) 6 times, 3ch, 1dc between top 2 dc rows at centre shoulder edge, 3ch, 1dc into end of next dc row, (3ch, miss next tr row, 1dc into end of next dc row) 6 times, turn.

Row 2: 3ch, 1dc into 1st loop, (3ch, 1dc) into each foll loop to end. Work another 3ch, 1dc into same end loop, turn. (15 loops).

Row 3: 3ch, 1dc into 1st loop, (3ch, 1dc) into each foll loop to end, turn.

Rows 4–9: Rep last row 6 times more. Do not turn at end of last row.

Row 10: Join sleeve into circle by working 1dc into 1st loop of row. 3ch (1st st), 1tr into same loop, 2tr into each foll loop to end, ss into top of 3ch.
Break yarn and fasten off.

LEFT SLEEVE

With RS facing, join yarn to 1st dc row of rem side of front bodice.

Rep from * on right sleeve.

UNDERLAY

Row 1: With RS facing, join yarn to corner dc at neck opening (skirt underlay side) and work down bodice edge as follows:
2ch (1st st), (2dc between end 2tr of next tr row, 1dc into end dc of next row) 6 times, 1dc into 1st loop at top of skirt, turn.

Row 2: Miss 1st st, 1dc into each foll st to end.
Break yarn and fasten off.

NECK

Row 1: With RS facing, join yarn to unworked corner st at neck opening, work 3ch (1st st), 1tr into each of next 10dc, work 6tr to front neck, 16tr across front neck, 6tr to back neck, 11tr to end, omitting underlay rows.
Break yarn and fasten off.

Join back of skirt from base to skirt underlay. Add 1 or 2 sts to secure underlay base on WS. Join sleeve sides, omitting the 1st 3 rows (underarm). Gather skirt slightly at underarms and sew gathered edges along remainder of opened-out sleeve sides.

Sew in all ends. Attach buttons to bodice underlay, and trimming to skirt edge.

MATINÉE COAT

✳

This is the perfect little jacket to keep baby nice and warm. Finish off with white or pastel ribbon, if you like.

MATERIALS

100g (3¾oz) Sirdar Snuggly 3 ply Yarn
Hook 3.00
0.5m (20in) narrow broderie anglaise trim for sleeves (optional)
2 small buttons
Matching sewing thread
Sewing needle

TENSION

23tr and 17 rows = 10cm (4in) sq, over patt

MEASUREMENTS

Width = 23cm (9in)
Back length = 23cm (9in)

BACK

Make 56ch.

Row 1: 1dc into 2nd ch from hook, 1dc into each foll ch to end, turn.

Row 2: 3ch (1st st), 1tr into each foll st to end, turn.

Row 3: 1ch (1st st), 1dc into each foll st to end, turn.

Rows 4–21: Rep last two rows 9 times more.

Row 22: As Row 2.

Row 23: 1ch, 1ss into each of 2nd and 3rd sts, 2ch

(1st dc), 1dc into each foll st to last 2sts, turn. (51sts).

Row 24: 3ch (1st st), tr2tog, 1tr into each foll st to last 3dc, tr2tog, 1tr into last dc, turn.

Row 25: 1ch (1st st), dc2tog, 1dc into each foll st to last 3sts, dc2tog, 1dc into last st, turn.

Rep last two rows until 19sts.

Row 40: As Row 24. Break yarn and fasten off.

◆
LEFT FRONT

Make 29ch.

Work Rows 1–22 as for back.

Row 23: 1ch, 1ss into each of 2nd and 3rd sts, 2ch (1st dc), 1dc into each foll st to end, turn. (26sts).

Row 24: 3ch (1st st), 1tr into each foll st to last 3dc, tr2tog, 1tr into last dc, turn.

Row 25: 1ch (1st st), dc2tog, 1dc into each foll st to end, turn.

Rows 26–31: Rep last two rows 3 times more.

Row 32: 3ch (1st st), tr2tog, 1tr into each foll st to last 3sts, tr2tog, 1tr into last st, turn.

Row 33: As Row 25. (15sts).

Rows 34–39: Rep last two rows 3 times more.

Row 40: 3ch (1st st), (tr2tog) twice, 1tr into last st. Break yarn and fasten off.

◆
RIGHT FRONT

Make 29ch.

Work Rows 1–22 as for back.

Row 23: 1ch (1st st), 1dc into each foll st to last 2sts, turn. (26sts).

Row 24: 3ch (1st st), tr2tog, 1tr into each foll st to end, turn.

Row 25: 1ch (1st st), 1dc into each foll st to last 3sts, dc2tog, 1dc into last st, turn.

Rows 26–31: Rep last two rows 3 times more.

Row 32: 3ch (1st st), tr2tog, 1tr into each foll st to last 3sts, tr2tog, 1tr into last st, turn.

Row 33: As Row 25. (15sts).

Rows 34–39: Rep last two rows 3 times more.

Row 40: 3ch (1st st), (tr2tog) twice, 1tr into last st. Break yarn and fasten off.

◆
SLEEVE

Make 28ch, fairly loosely.

Row 1: 1dc into 2nd ch from hook, 1dc into each foll ch to end, turn.

Row 2: 3ch (1st st), 2tr into next st, 1tr into each foll st to last 2sts, 2tr into next st, 1tr into last st, turn.

Row 3: 1ch (1st st), 1dc into each foll st to end, turn.

Row 4: 3ch (1st st), 1tr into each foll st to end, turn.

Rows 5 and 6: Rep last two rows once more.

Row 7: As Row 3.

Row 8: As Row 2.

Rows 9–12: Rep Rows 3 and 4 twice more.

Row 13: As Row 3.

Row 14: As Row 2.

Rows 15–18: Rep Rows 3 and 4 twice more.

Row 19: As Row 3.

Row 20: As Row 2.

Row 21: 1ch, 1ss into each of 2nd and 3rd sts, 2ch (1st dc), 1dc into each foll st to last 2sts, turn. (31sts).

Row 22: 3ch (1st st), tr2tog, 1tr into each foll st to last 3dc, tr2tog, 1tr into last dc, turn.

Row 23: 1ch (1st st), 1dc into each foll st to end, turn.

Row 24: 3ch (1st st), tr2tog, 1tr into each foll st to last 3sts, tr2tog, 1tr into last st, turn.

Rep last two rows until 13sts. Break yarn and fasten off. Make another sleeve the same.

On WS, butt together raglan edges of front, sleeve, back, sleeve, front, and sew together in turn. (Either side of patt can be chosen as RS.) Sew sleeve and side seams.

◆
NECK

With WS facing, join yarn to top of 1st tr at opening edge of L front neck.

Row 1: 1ch (1st st), 1dc into each of next 3tr, work 7dc evenly across sleeve top, 17dc across back, 7dc evenly across 2nd sleeve top, 4dc along top of R front neck, turn.

Row 2: Miss 1st st, 1htr into next st, 1tr into each st to last 2sts of row, decreasing 1 st at centre back, 1htr into next st, 1ss into last st. Break yarn and fasten off.

With RS facing, join yarn to base st at opening edge of R front, work 3dc around end tr (stem) of each tr row up to neck, 1dc between missed st and 1st htr of neck, 1dc between htr and next tr, 1dc into each tr around neck, to last htr. Work 1dc between last tr and htr, 1dc between htr and ss, 3dc around end tr (stem) of each tr row to base of L front. Break yarn and fasten off. Sew in ends. Attach buttons. Sew trimming to RS of sleeve edges and fold back, adding one or two sts to secure.

BONNET

❋❋

This light, warm bonnet is perfect for the bonny baby in your life. The back is worked first from base to top, then the sides are added in one piece. Complete the picture with a small frill round the face and neck edges.

◆

MATERIALS

50g (2oz) Sirdar Snuggly 3 ply Yarn
Hook 3.00
0.75m × 2.5cm (30 × 1in) ribbon
Matching sewing thread
Sewing needle

◆

TENSION

23tr and 17 rows = 10cm (4in) sq
Over loop patt, 10dc + 9 loops and
26 rows = 10cm (4in) sq

◆

MEASUREMENTS

Face edge = 32.5cm (13in)
Back length = 13 × 13cm (5¼ × 5¼in) widest part

◆

BACK

Make 21ch.
Row 1: 1tr into 4th ch from hook, 1tr into each foll ch to end, turn.
Row 2: 1ch (1st dc), 2dc into next st, (1dc into each of next 7sts, 2dc into next st) twice, 1dc, turn.
Row 3: 3ch (1st tr), 1tr into each foll st to end, turn.
Row 4: 1ch (1st dc), 2dc into next st, 1dc into each of next 7sts, 2dc into next st, 1dc into each of next 2sts, 2dc into next st, 1dc into each of next 7sts, 2dc into next st, 1dc, turn.
Row 5: As Row 3.
Row 6: 1ch (1st dc), 2dc into next st, 1dc into each of next 8sts, 2dc into next st, 1dc into each of next 4sts, 2dc into next st, 1dc into each of next 8sts, 2dc into next st, 1dc, turn.
Row 7: As Row 3.
Row 8: 1ch (1st dc), 1dc into each foll st to end, turn.
Row 9: As Row 3.
Rows 10 and 11: Rep last 2 rows once more.

Row 12: 1ch (1st dc), dc next 2sts tog, 1dc into each foll st to last 3sts, dc2tog, 1dc, turn.

Row 13: As Row 3.

Row 14: As Row 8.

Row 15: As Row 3.

Row 16: As Row 12.

Row 17: As Row 3.

Row 18: 1ch (1st dc), dc2tog, 1dc into each of next 4sts, dc2tog, 1dc into each of next 8sts, dc2tog, 1dc into each of next 4sts, dc2tog, 1dc, turn. (22sts).

Row 19: As Row 3.

Row 20: 1ch (1st dc), dc2tog, (1dc into each of next 4sts, dc2tog) 3 times, 1dc, turn.

Row 21: 2ch (1st htr), tr2tog, 1tr into each foll st to last 3sts, tr2tog, 1htr, turn.

Row 22: 1ch (1st dc), dc2tog, (1dc into each of next 2sts, dc2tog) 3 times, 1dc. (12sts).

Break yarn and fasten off.

•

SIDE

Begin by working loops around edge of back, excluding base.

Row 1: With preferred side facing (RS), join yarn between 2 end trs of 1st row.

Make 3ch, 1dc into same sp, *(3ch,1dc) into each edge sp of next 5 tr rows, 3ch, (1dc,3ch,1dc = inc loop) into next tr row, (3ch,1dc) into each of next 2 tr rows, 3ch, inc loop in next tr row, 3ch, (1dc, 3ch) into next end htr row.

Across top 12sts, work (1dc,3ch) into 2nd, 5th, 8th and 11th sts.

Cont along rem edge to base, matching 1st side, turn. (31 loops).

Row 2: 3ch, 1dc into 1st loop, *3ch, 1dc into next loop. Rep from * to end, working one inc loop at centre top, turn.

Rows 3–20: Omitting an inc, rep last row 18 times more (approx 7cm (2½in)).

Row 21: As patt but work 2ch instead of 3ch loops, turn.

Row 22: 2ch, 1dc into 1st loop, 2ch, *1dc into next dc, 2ch.

Rep from * to end, but work a dc into last 2ch loop, turn.

Rows 23 and 24: Work the (3ch,1dc) patt into each loop to end, turn.

Row 25: As patt but work 4ch instead of 3ch loops, turn.

Row 26: (WS facing) 3ch, *(1dc,3ch) 3 times into next loop. Rep from * to end, omitting final 3ch. Temporarily unhook loop. With RS facing, fold frill at Rows 21–22 (2ch rows) onto RS of bonnet. Reinsert hook and secure corner of frill in position by working a ss at end of Row 16 (approx). Turn.

Row 27: (WS facing) 2ch (1st st), make 9dc evenly along neck edge of side, to base of back (working into the sps), 11dc evenly across base ch edge, picking up single sts of base ch, 10dc evenly into sps along neck edge of rem side until equivalent place is reached as at beg of this row. Fold frill onto RS, and attach corner with a ss, as on prev row, turn.

Row 28: 1dc into last dc made, 1htr into next dc, (1ch,1tr) twice into each foll dc to last 2sts, 1ch, 1htr into next st, 1ss into 2ch. Break yarn. Fasten off. Insert a length of ribbon through each hole at end of frill, and stitch securely in place.

BABY SHAWL

✳✳✳

A light, warm shawl with extra frilly corners. A pattern of feathers and picot festoons combine to make a deep, decorative border.

•

MATERIALS

200g (7¼oz) Sirdar Snuggly 3 ply Yarn
Hook 3.00

•

TENSION

Over main section loop patt, 10dc+9 loops and 26 rows = 10cm (4in) sq

•

MEASUREMENTS

Main section = 70cm (27½in) sq
Border = Approx 12cm (4½in) deep

The Nursery

METHOD

Make 134ch, loosely.

Row 1: 1dc into 4th ch from hook, *3ch, miss next ch, 1dc into next ch.

Rep from * to end, turn. (66 loops).

Row 2: 3ch, 1dc into 1st loop, *3ch, 1dc into next loop.

Rep from * to end, turn.

Rep last row until fabric is square. Turn.

BORDER

Round 1: 1st side − 7ch (dtr+3ch), (1dtr,3ch) 5 times into 1st loop (corner), miss next loop, (1dc,3ch) into each of next 2 loops, *miss next loop, (1dtr,3ch) 4 times into next loop, miss next loop, (1dc,3ch) into each of next 2 loops.

Rep from * to last 2 loops of side, miss next loop, (1dtr,3ch) 6 times into next loop (corner).

(12 'fans' and 13 loops between corners.)

2nd side − (last corner loop = 1st row) 1dc into loop at edge of 5th row from 1st side, 3ch, 1dc into loop at edge of 7th row from 1st side, 3ch.

Cont by making altogether 12 fans and 13 loops evenly along 2nd side, to match 1st side, initially by pinning 1st side approx 2cm (³⁄₄in) below edge on front of 2nd side and following fan and loop positions.

After the final 3ch, work (1dtr,3ch) 6 times into last loop for corner.

3rd side − miss next loop, (1dc,3ch) into each of next 2 loops.

Rep from * as 1st side, completing foll corner.

4th side − work to match 2nd side. After final 3ch, ss into 4th of 7ch.

Round 2: Ss into next sp, 7ch (dtr+3ch), (1dtr,3ch) twice and 1dtr all into same sp, **(1dtr, 3ch,1dtr = 'V') into next sp, (1ttr,3ch) 3 times and 1ttr all into next sp at centre corner, 'V' into next sp, (1dtr,3ch) 4 times into next sp.

Make a picot (= make 1tr, inserting hook through top loop and out of top left stem of last dtr made).

(Miss next dtr,3ch,dc), (1dtr,3ch) twice into next loop (of 13 loops), picot, *(1dtr,3ch) 4 times into next fan centre loop, picot (1dtr,3ch) twice into next loop (of 13 loops), picot.

Rep from * to next corner, (miss next dc,3ch,dtr), (1dtr,3ch) 3 times and 1dtr all into 1st of next 5 corner sps.

Rep from ** along rem sides to 1st corner, ending with picot. Ss into 4th of 7ch.

Round 3: (Missing next sp) work 5ss to foll sp (=centre of 1st fan of corner), 7ch (1dtr,3ch) 3 times into same sp, **picot, (miss next dtr,3ch, 2dtr), (1dtr,3ch) twice into next 'V' sp, picot (miss next dtr, ttr, 3ch, ttr), work (1ttr,3ch) 4 times into centre sp of ttr fan at corner, picot (into ttr).

(Miss next ttr,3ch,ttr,dtr), (1dtr,3ch) twice into next 'V' sp, picot, *(1dtr,3ch) 4 times into centre sp of next fan, picot, miss next sp, (1dtr,3ch) twice into 'V' sp foll next picot, picot.

Rep from * to last picot of side, (1dtr,3ch) 4 times into centre sp of dtr fan at beg of corner.

Rep from ** along rem sides to beg of 1st corner, ending with picot. Ss into 4th of 7ch.

Round 4: (Missing next sp) work 5ss to centre sp of 1st fan of corner, 7ch, (1dtr,3ch) 3 times into same sp, **2 picots (=1tr into last dtr or ttr as before, 3ch, 1tr through top and side of last tr made), miss next sp and picot, (1dtr,3ch) twice into next 'V' sp, 2 picots, (miss next picot and sp), work (1ttr,3ch) 4 times into centre sp of ttr fan at corner, 2 picots.

Miss next sp and picot, (1dtr,3ch) twice into next 'V' sp, 2 picots, miss next picot and sp, *(1dtr, 3ch) 4 times into centre sp of next fan, picot, (1dtr, 3ch) twice into 'V' sp foll next picot, picot.

Rep from * to dtr fan at beg of next corner, (1dtr,3ch) 4 times into centre sp of fan.

Rep from ** along rem sides to beg of 1st corner, ending with picot.

Ss into 4th of 7ch.

Round 5: Cont patt as Rnd 4 but instead of 2 picots in a row, work 3 picots.

Round 6: Cont patt as Rnd 4 but instead of 2 picots in a row, work 4 picots.

Round 7: (Missing next sp), work 5ss to centre sp of 1st fan of corner, 7ch, 1tr into 4th ch from hook, (1dtr,3ch,picot) 5 times into same sp, **add 2 picots onto last picot, (1dtr,3ch,picot) 4 times into next 'V' sp, 2 picots (=3 in a row), (1ttr,3ch,picot) 6 times into centre corner sp, 2 picots.

Work (1dtr,3ch, picot) 4 times into next 'V' sp, 2 picots, *(1dtr,3ch,picot) 6 times into next fan centre, (1dtr,3ch,picot) 4 times into next 'V' sp.

Rep from * to last single picot of side, (1dtr,3ch, picot) 6 times into next fan centre.

Rep from ** along rem sides to 1st corner, ss into 4th of 7ch.

99

Christmas Fairy (page 106) with a variety of
Christmas tree decorations (pages 102–5)

CHAPTER EIGHT
Celebration

RIBBON

This looped ribbon, worked in a glittery yarn, has many uses – including Christmas tree decorating, parcel wrapping, and holding Christmas cards – so make plenty!

◆

MATERIALS

Twilleys Gold Dust (2 ply)
Hooks 2.00 and 6.00
Sewing needle

◆

METHOD

To make approx 30cm (12in) of ribbon, double 3m (3¼yd) of yarn. With 6.00 hook, make 45ch (or any odd no) with this doubled yarn.

From now on use the 2.00 hook and single yarn from the spool; make 1 more ch st.

Treat each ch st of doubled yarn as consisting of 6 strands, and insert hook so that 3 strands are above and 3 strands are below the hook.

Row 1: Into 2nd ch from hook, work 6htr, *1ss into next ch, 6htr into foll ch.
Rep from * to end.

Row 2: With slip-knot behind, work a further 6htr into same end ch.

Cont along opp side of ch length, repeating from * as for prev row, until end. Ss into 1st st.

Sew in ends.

BELL

Simple double crochet, a small amount of stitchery with a sewing needle, and a lovely glittery yarn, all combine to make this little bell.

◆

MATERIALS

Approx 18m (20yd) Twilleys Gold Dust (2 ply)
Hook 2.00
Sewing needle

◆

TENSION

1st 4 rounds = 2.5cm (1in) dia

◆

HEIGHT

6cm (2¼in)

◆

METHOD

Leaving a 15cm (6in) end of yarn, make 4ch. Join with ss into circle.

Round 1: 1ch, 8dc into circle, ss into 1st dc.

Round 2: 1ch (1st dc), dc twice into each foll st to end, 1dc into st at base of 1st dc, ss into 1st dc. (16sts).

Round 3: 1ch (1st dc), 2dc into next st, *1dc into next st, 2dc into foll st.
Rep from * to end, ss into 1st dc.

Round 4: Work 24ss to end.

Round 5: 1ch (1st dc), work 23 fairly loose dc under last round and between dc of Rnd 3, enclosing ss's of Rnd 4. Ss into 1st dc.

Round 6: 1ch (1st dc), dc to end, ss into 1st dc. (24sts).

Omit ch and ss on foll rounds. Use marker to indicate round ends.

Round 7: Dc to end.

Round 8: Inc 1dc in 1st st, dc to end, working on outside.

Round 9: Dc to end, inc 1dc in 10th st.

Round 10: Dc to end, inc 1dc in 19th st.

Rounds 11 and 12: Dc to end.

Round 13: Dc to end, inc 1dc in 8th st.

Round 14: Dc to end, inc 1dc in 17th st.

Round 15: Dc to end, inc 1dc in 28th st.

Round 16: Dc to end, inc 1dc in every 5th st. (36sts).

Round 17: Dc to end.

Round 18: Dc to end but inc 1dc in 3rd and every foll 6th st, ending with 3dc.

Round 19: Dc to end.

Round 20: Dc to end but miss 3rd and every foll 6th st, ending with 3dc. Work 1ss to finish off.

Break yarn. Fold final round to inside. Using the same yarn, oversew close upright sts over bell edge, and Rnd 5 at edge of top circle.

Wind yarn 6 times around finger. Tightly button-hole-st around this circle until firm.

Trim and fold double the 15cm (6in) end to fit inside for the 'clapper'. Double-knot one end and stitch other end to inside. Sew on the handle, winding yarn a few times around handle base while stitching.

CHRISTMAS BALL

✳

Make this lovely 3-D decoration in metallic thread to hang where it will catch the light.

◆

MATERIALS

Approx 12g (½oz) Twilleys Goldfingering (3 ply)
Hook 2.50
Sewing needle
Lightweight stuffing

◆

TENSION

1st 5 rounds = 4cm (1½in) dia

◆

HEIGHT

Approx 6cm (2½in)

◆

METHOD

Make 4ch. Join with ss into circle.

Round 1: Work 8dc into circle.

Round 2: 2dc into each st.

Round 3: (1dc into next st, 2dc into foll st) 8 times.

Round 4: Dc to end.

Round 5: (1dc into each of next 5sts, 2dc into foll st) 4 times.

Round 6: (1dc into each of next 6sts, 2dc into foll st) 4 times.

Round 7: 1dc into each of next 3sts, 2dc into foll st, (1dc into each of next 7sts, 2dc into foll st) 3 times, 1dc into each of next 4sts. (36sts).

Round 8: Dc to end.

Round 9: (1dc into each of next 8sts, 2dc into foll st) 4 times.

Rounds 10 and 11: Dc to end.

Round 12: 10ch, miss next 10sts, dc to end.

Round 13: 1dc into each ch st, dc to end.

Round 14: Dc to end.

Round 15: (1dc into each of next 9sts, miss next st) 3 times, 1dc into each of next 8sts, miss next st, 1dc.

Round 16: Dc to end.

Round 17: 1dc into each of next 4sts, miss next st, (1dc into each of next 8sts, miss next st) 3 times, 1dc into each of next 4sts.

Round 18: (1dc into each of next 7sts, miss next st) 3 times, 1dc into each of next 6sts, miss next st, 1dc.

Round 19: (1dc into each of next 6sts, miss next st) 3 times, 1dc into each of next 5sts, miss next st, 1dc.

Round 20: (1dc into each of next 2sts, miss next st) 7 times, 1dc into next st, miss next st, 1dc.

Round 21: (1dc into each of next 4sts, miss next st) 3 times, 1dc.

Rounds 22–25: Dc to end.

Round 26: Dc to last st, 1ss.

Leaving approx 30cm (12in) of thread, break yarn. Tease out stuffing and fill loosely (see below). Close side opening. Fold final 2 rounds to inside top and with the same yarn stitch across neck. Leave 20cm (8in) for loop. Decorate as desired.

To maintain the shape, the opening for stuffing is made at the side

CHRISTMAS TREE DECORATIONS

These delightful little tree trimmings are quickly and easily made, and are ideal for finishing up scraps of yarn and oddments of decoration. Try making a few for a pre-Christmas sale of work. They'll be snapped up!

◆

MATERIALS

Yarn oddments (red and white for Boot, white cotton for Snow Crystal)
Hooks in suitable sizes
Beads, sequins, metallic thread or other decorations
Card for stiffening (optional)
All-purpose adhesive
Fabric stiffener (optional)

◆

MEASUREMENTS

Depends on yarn and hook size. Heart in DK with a suitable hook size = approx 8 × 7cm (3 × 2½in)

HEART ✷ ✷

Using main colour (MC) yarn , make 3ch. Join with ss into circle.

Round 1: 1ch, 7dc into circle, ss into 1st dc. (7sts).
Round 2: 1ch (1st st), 2dc into each of next 6sts, 1dc into ss at base of 1st st, ss into 1st st. (14sts).
Round 3: 2ch (1st st), 4tr into next st, miss next st, 1dc into next st, miss next st, 4tr into next st, 1htr into each of next 3sts, 3htr into next st, 1tr into next st, 3htr into next st, 1htr into each of next 2sts, ss into top of 2ch.
Round 4: 1ch (1st st), 1dc into each of next 2sts (2htr, 1tr) into next st, (1htr, 1dc) into next st, 1dc into next st, (1dc, 1htr) into next st, (1tr, 2htr) into next st, 1dc into each of next 3sts, dc2tog, 1dc into each of next 4sts, 2ch, 1dc into each of next 5sts.
With contrasting colour (CC) yarn, ss into 1st st.
Round 5: Using same CC yarn, work 2ch (1st st) 1dc into each of next 3sts, 2dc into each of next 3sts, 1dc into next st, 1ss into next st at centre bow, 1dc into next st, 2dc into each of next 3sts, 1dc into each of next 9sts, (1dc, 2ch, 1dc) into 2ch loop, 1dc into each of next 5dc.
With MC yarn, ss into top of 1st 2ch.
Break off CC yarn.

Round 6: 2ch, (1ss into next st, 1ch) 9 times, 1ss into next st, miss next ss, (1ss into next st, 1ch) 17 times, 1ss into 2ch loop, 2ch, (1ss into next dc, 1ch) 6 times, 1ss into 1st of 2ch at start of round.
Fasten off.
Worked in a DK yarn, the heart also makes a sweet pocket for a little girl's jumper.

◆

2–D BALL ✸

Make 6ch. Join with ss into circle.
Round 1: 3ch (1st tr), 15tr into circle, ss into top of 3ch.
Round 2: 3ch (1st tr), 1tr into same place as 3ch, 2tr into each of next 15tr, ss into top of 3ch.
Round 3: 3ch (1st tr), 2tr into next st, *1tr into next st, 2tr into next st.
Rep from * to end, ss into top of 3ch.
Round 4: 1ch (1st dc), dc to end, ss into 1st dc.
Round 5: 3ch (1st tr), 2tr into each of next 2sts, 1tr into next st, turn.
Round 6: 2ch (1st dc), 5dc to end.
Fasten off.

◆

BOOT ✸

With white yarn, make 15ch. Join with ss into circle.
Round 1: (RS) 3ch (1st tr), 1tr into each foll ch to end, ss into top of 3ch. (RS is outside.)
Round 2: 2ch (1st htr), 1htr into each foll st to end. Break off white yarn, ss with red yarn into top of 2ch. (15htr).
Flatten work so that last ss made (above 1st htr) is on its own at rhs.
Row 1: Make 1ch. Through both layers work 1dc into each of rem 7 htr pairs, turn (see below).
Row 2: 1ch (1st dc), 1dc into each of next 6sts – leave last ch unworked, turn.

Work 1dc into each of seven pairs of stitches

Row 3: 1ch (1st dc), 6dc to end, turn.
Rep last row 3 times more.
Row 7: Make 5ch. Into 2nd ch from hook, work 1dc, 3dc along remainder of ch, 1dc into each of next 7sts to end, turn.
Row 8: 1ch (1st dc), 1dc into each of next 6sts, dc2tog, dc to end, (10dc) turn.
Rows 9–11: 1ch (1st dc), dc to end, turn.
Row 12: 1dc into each of the 10sts – inc 1dc in last st. Do not turn. Cont around toe, 1dc into toe-side centre, 1ss into 5ch-end st of Row 7.
Break yarn and fasten off. Sew in ends.
Twist a length of red yarn and cotton together, fold in half to form thin cord (see Techniques) and thread right around and between Rnds 1 and 2. Tie ends into a tiny bow.

♦

SNOW CRYSTAL ✿✿

Make 6ch. Join with ss into circle.
Round 1: 3ch (1st tr), work 23tr into circle, ss into top of 3ch. (24tr.)
Round 2: *3ch (1st tr), 1tr into next st, make 19ch, 1tr into each of next 2tr, 2ch.
Replace 1st 3ch with 1tr into next st, and rep from * to end, ss into top of 3ch.
Round 3: *Working around next 19ch sts: 3ch, (1ss,3ch,1tr) into 3rd ch st, (1ss,3ch,2tr) into 6th ch st, 1ss into 9th ch st, 2ch, 1htr into 10th ch st,

2ch, 1ss into 11th ch st, (2tr,3ch,1ss) into 14th ch st, (1tr,3ch,1ss) into 17th ch st, 3ch.
(Miss both the remainder of 19ch and tr beneath), 1ss into next tr, 1ss into 1st of next 2ch, 1ss into sp of same 2ch, make 24ch.
Into 14th ch from hook, (1ss,15ch,1ss,13ch,1ss).
Work 10ss along remainder of 24ch, 1ss into 2nd of 2ch at base of 24ch just made, 1ss into next tr.
Rep from * to end, omitting last ss at end of round.
Fasten off. Press. Attach a sequin back and front at centre and at 3-petal ss's and apply a fabric stiffener, or stick or sew to hexagonal card with the sequins fixed to one side only (see below).

The crystal can either be stiffened, or fixed to an hexagonal piece of card as shown

CHRISTMAS FAIRY

✳✳✳

This lovely fairy is a must for the top of your Christmas tree. You will probably find the odds and ends of cloth (old sheeting is ideal) and yarn you need to make her in your work basket. Remember, she isn't suitable as a toy for small children.

◆

MATERIALS

50g (2oz) White DMC Cebelia
No 10 Crochet Cotton
(for wings, leg and
arm covering)
Hook 1.50
Approx 16m (17½yd) silver lurex
yarn (wings and decoration)
5 × 18cm (7in) lengths white wire
– paper-clip strength (wings, dress
hoop, halo, wand)
Any other colour wire can be
painted with white correction fluid
All-purpose adhesive
3cm (1¼in) dia piece of eggshell
and felt pens (face)
Grey or brown embroidery silk
(leg division)
White sewing thread
(dress and dress hoop)
34 × 21cm (13 × 8in) white
sheeting (dress)
2.5cm (1in) thick foam sponge
19 × 10cm (7½ × 4in)
(body)
2cm (¾in) silver tinsel (wand star)
Small amount white 4-ply or
DK yarn (hair)
Sewing needle
Optional:
Extras for dress
decoration – sequins, beads, net

◆

HEIGHT

Approx 20cm (8in)

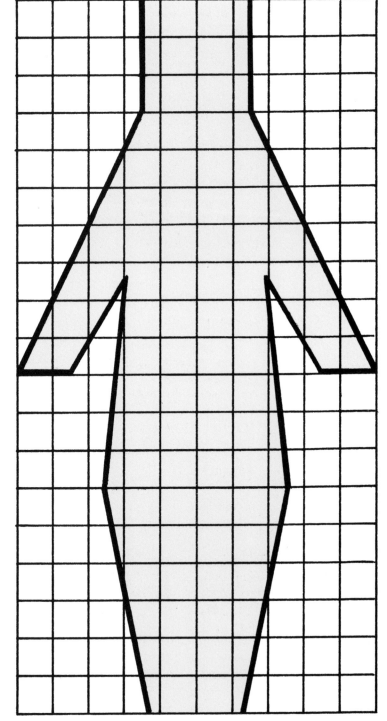

Cut out the doll from a piece of foam sponge 19 x 10cm (7½ x 4in)

METHOD

Make paper pattern from diagram on page 106. Cut out doll in foam. Snip .25cm (⅛in) into foam across tops of front and back legs. Trim off this .25cm (⅛in) excess foam down to base, tapering slightly inwards (see below left).

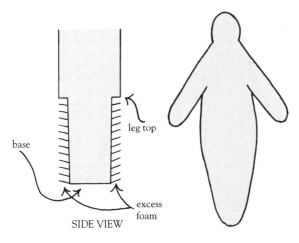

base

leg top

excess foam

SIDE VIEW

Trim away some foam to distinguish the legs (left)
Completed body, after shaping (right)

Round off all edges, including corners of head top, tips of hands and feet, and trunk to legs.
Snip 1cm (½in) under arms, to lengthen (see above right).
(Front and back leg tops should each measure approx 4.5cm (1¾in) across.)

LEG COVERING

(Feet to waist. Make 2)
With crochet cotton, make 38ch.
Row 1: 1dc into 2nd ch from hook, 1dc into each foll ch to end, turn.
Row 2: 2ch (count 2ch as 1st st of rows), 2dc into next st, 1dc into each foll st to end, turn. (38sts).
Row 3: 2ch, 1dc into each foll st to last 2sts, 2dc into next st, 1dc into last st, turn.
Rep last 2 rows once more.
Row 6: 2ch, 1dc into each of next 21sts, 1htr into each foll st to end, turn.
Row 7: 2ch, 1htr into each of next 19sts, 1dc into each foll st to end, turn.
Row 8: 2ch, 1dc into each of next 20sts, 1htr into each foll st to end, turn.
Row 9: 2ch, 1dc into each foll st to end, turn.

Row 10: As Row 8.
Row 11: As Row 7.
Row 12: As Row 6.
Row 13: As Row 9.
Row 14: As Row 9 but dec 1 st at beg of row.
Row 15: As Row 9 but dec 1 st at end of row.
Rep last 2 rows once more. (37sts).
Break yarn and fasten off.
Leaving shorter straight edges open (waist), backstitch curved ends tog, turn to RS, fit onto doll and oversew sides tog. With 3 strands of embroidery silk, tightly stitch through leg coverings and foam a dividing line for legs (see below). Separate feet slightly with a final oversewn st.

Cover doll's arms and legs. Divide legs with a line of stitches down the centre

ARM AND HAND COVERING

(Make 2)
With crochet cotton, make 16ch.
Row 1: 1dc into 2nd ch from hook, 1dc into each foll ch to end, turn.
Row 2: 2ch (count 2ch as 1st st of rows), 2dc into next st, 1dc into each foll st to end, turn. (16sts.)
Row 3: 2ch, 1dc into each foll st to last 2sts, 2dc into next st, 1dc into last st, turn.
Row 4: As Row 2.
Row 5: 2ch, 1htr into each of next 8sts, 1dc into each foll st to end, turn.
Rows 6–13: 2ch, 1dc into each foll st to end, turn.
Row 14: 2ch, 1dc into each of next 8sts, 1htr into each foll st to end, turn.
Row 15: As Row 6 but dec 1 st at end of row.
Row 16: As Row 6 but dec 1 st at beg of row.

Row 17: As Row 6 but dec 1 st at end of row.
Row 18: As Row 6 (15sts).
Break yarn and fasten off.
Fold sides tog to form glove. Using the same yarn, backstitch curved end, turn to RS, fit glove onto doll and stitch sides (see page 107 right).

Dressed doll

◆

DRESS

Form one piece of wire into a circle, overlapping ends by 1cm (½in). Place a dab of glue over ends and wind the sewing thread tightly around, to secure. Join together two short edges of sheeting with a felled seam (see below).

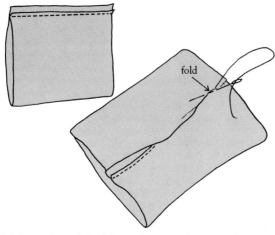

Make a tube with the fabric. Place one edge below the other to start a felled seam. Fold over the deeper edge and stitch down

Turn 1cm (½in) of one raw edge (neck) to WS, and tack down. Make a 0.75cm (⅓in) hem on RS with rem raw edge, enclosing hoop between two circles of small sts.
Place dress onto doll with seam down the back and wire circle at base. Gather neck and secure. Remove tacking. Adjust dress gathers evenly around body. With arms flat against body, cut two small horizontal slits in dress just above wrist fronts, to bring hands through. Stitch openings to wrists. Cover with small chains, as bracelets, made with the lurex yarn. Separate sleeves from bodice with a few sts in cotton thread.
Lift hoop upwards, outside dress, to hip level. Even out gathers. Squeeze together back and front of hoop and bend sides slightly upwards. Glue or sew narrow waves of a lurex chain around dress to conceal hoop stitching (see above right). Add extra dress decoration if required.

FACE AND DECORATION

Form curls with 4-ply or DK yarn wound over the end of a crochet hook, and carefully slide onto dabs of glue applied on head. Leave out curls nearest face until face is in position. Apply a little glue over completed curls to set, and shine, hair. Affix face (as close to a 3cm (1¼in) dia circle of eggshell as is possible) onto doll with glue, and position final curls. Add light features with felt pens.
Glue or sew on small lurex chains for necklaces. Embroider a silver star onto point of each foot.

◆

WINGS

(Make 2)
Join ends of a piece of wire, as on dress hoop, and shape as shown below. (If used, omit correction fluid for wings, as wire is concealed.)
Round 1: Using white crochet cotton, work 114 dc evenly around wire, leaving join until last. Ss into 1st dc.

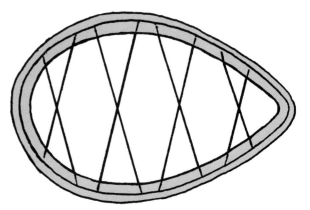

Wing shape, with crosses in silver yarn for decoration

Round 2: Change to silver yarn and work 1dc into every alternate st. Ss into 1st dc.

Round 3: (White) 1dc into each st to end but inc 2sts at bend and inc 12 more sts evenly over round. Ss into 1st dc.

Round 4: (Silver) 5ch, miss next st, *1dc into next st, 4ch, miss next st.

Rep from * to end, ss into 1st of 5ch. Break yarn and sew in ends.

Use silver yarn to decorate with crosses as shown on p108. To stiffen, paint first two rounds, and crosses, with 2 teaspoons of sugar dissolved in approx a teaspoon of boiling water. Allow to dry thoroughly.

Shape halo from another piece of wire (see right). Taking care not to damage face, push (slightly slanting to the back) through back curls – allowing end to rest at back of neck. Glue point of entry through curls. To make the wand, fold wire in half at 10cm (4in) from one end. Twist, leaving a thin loop at fold. Glue tinsel through loop (see right). Stitch onto hand. Stitch wings into foam, to centre back of doll.

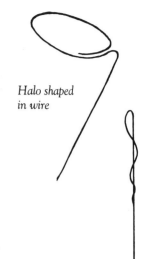

Halo shaped in wire

Wand showing loop for tinsel

SNOWMAN

*

Made all-in-one, this snowman has a detachable base which makes him easy to launder and keep snowy white.

MATERIALS

100g (3¾oz) Jarol Supersaver White DK yarn
Hooks 4.50 for snowman, hat and scarf;
3.50 for nose
Yarn oddments for nose, scarf and black for hat, eyes, mouth and buttons
10cm (4in) dia circle of stiff card for snowman base
12cm (5in) dia circle of white fabric to cover card
3.5cm (1½in) dia circle of card for hat
Washable stuffing
Wool needle
Sewing needle
Pencil

TENSION

1st 9 rounds = 10cm (4in) dia

HEIGHT

Approx 20cm (8in)

BODY

With 4.50 hook, make 4ch. Join with ss into circle.

Round 1: 8dc into circle.

Round 2: 2dc into each st to end.

Round 3: *2dc into next st, 1dc into foll st. Rep from * to end.

Round 4: *1dc into each of next 3sts, 2dc into next st. Rep from * to end. (30sts).

Round 5: *2dc into next st, 1dc into each of next 5sts. Rep from * to end.

Round 6: Dc to end.

Round 7: *1dc into each of next 4sts, 2dc into next st. Rep from * to end.

Rounds 8 and 9: Rep Rnds 5 and 6 once more.

Round 10: 1dc into each of next 4sts, *2dc into next st, 1dc into each of next 6sts.

Rep from * to last 3sts, 2dc into next st, 2dc. (56sts).

Round 11: As Rnd 6.

Rounds 12–30: Continuing in dc, dec 1 st in varying positions over each of the next 18 rounds, and 2sts on the foll round (Rnd 30). After a few rounds, temporarily hold stitch on hook with safety pin and stitch fabric to RS base with a small hem enclosing the 10cm (4in) dia circle of card.

Round 31: Make 16ch for first arm, 1dc into next st on body, work 17 more dc on body, 16ch for other arm, 1dc into each of next 3sts on body, dc2tog, work 13dc to end.

Round 32: 1dc into each of 1st 16ch, 1dc into each of next 2sts, dc2tog, dc to next 16ch, 1dc into each ch st, dc to end. (66sts).

Rounds 33–40: Incorporating arms, work 8 rounds of dc, dec 1 st in varying positions over each round on body front and back but not arms, 8 decs in all.

Round 41: Dc to end, dec 1 st on both body front and back. (56sts).

Round 42: *Miss next 21sts, (2dc into next st, 1dc into each of next 2sts) twice, 2dc into next st. Rep from * once more. (20sts).

Round 43: *1dc into next st, 2dc into next st. Rep from * to end. (30sts).

Round 44: Dc to end.

Round 45: *1dc into each of next 4sts, 2dc into next st. Rep from * to end.

Round 46–51: Dc to end.

Round 52: *Miss next st, 1dc into each of next 5sts. Rep from * to end.

Rounds 53 and 54: Dc to end.

Round 55: *Miss next st, 1dc into each of next 4sts. Rep from * to end.

Round 56: *Miss next st, 1dc into each of next 3sts. Rep from * to end.

Round 57: *Miss next st, 1dc into each of next 2sts. Rep from * to end.

Round 58: *Miss next st, 1dc into foll st. Rep from * to end. Break yarn.

Darn in end, closing hole at top of head.

On RS, ladder-stitch underarms, tucking corners inside to make rounded ends. Beg with head, stuff completely, and then gather neck a little with some running stitches. Close above arms, again tucking corners inside.

◆

HAT

Rounds 1–3: Work as for Snowman to the end of Rnd 3.

Rounds 4–8: Dc to end.

Round 9: (2dc into next st, 1dc into each of next 7sts) 3 times.

Rounds 10 and 11: Dc to end.

Round 12: *1dc into next st, 2dc into next st. Rep from * to last st, 1dc.

Round 13: Dc to end.

Round 14: Ss to end.

Break yarn.

◆

HAT LINING

Work as for Snowman to end of Rnd 3.

Break yarn. Fit 3.5cm (1½in) dia circle of card into hat and stitch in lining to cover.

◆

NOSE

With 3.50 hook, make 3ch. Join with ss into circle.

Round 1: 6dc into circle.

Round 2: (1dc into each of next 2sts, 2dc into next st) twice.

Round 3: Dc to end, make 1ss.

Stitch nose onto face.

◆

SCARF

With 4.50 hook, make 47ch.

Work into single uppermost loops only on all rows.

Row 1: 1dc into 2nd ch from hook, 1dc into each foll ch to end, turn.

Rows 2–4: 2ch (1st dc), 1dc into each foll st to end. Break yarn.

To make two tiny white snowball bobbles for scarf ends, place approx 18cm (7in) yarn along the length of a pencil. Wind more yarn around the pencil and length of yarn, 30 or 40 turns, staying around the centre of the pencil, and cut. Holding short yarn ends, slide off pencil and tie very securely. Cut through loops and trim.

Gather scarf ends and attach bobbles Embroider eyes, mouth and 3 buttons down front to complete.

BASKET

✳

A charming and unusual gift, you could line this pretty basket with a circle of net or pretty fabric and fill it with home-made candies, or make a dainty arrangement with dried, silk or even fresh flowers in florist's foam on a lid, to pop inside.

◆

MATERIALS

20g (1oz) Coats Crochet Cotton No 5
Hook 1.75
2m (2yd) matching DK yarn for cord handle
80 × 0.75cm (30 × ¼in) ribbon
Fabric stiffener

◆

TENSION/MEASUREMENTS

Base = 8cm (3in) dia
Side = 3–4cm (1¼–1½in) high
Top = 14cm (5½in) dia

◆

BASE

Make 5ch. Join with ss into circle.
Round 1: 3ch (1st tr), 14tr into circle, ss into top of 3ch.
Round 2: 3ch (1st tr), 1tr into same place as 3ch, 2tr into each foll st to end, ss into top of 3ch. (30sts).
Round 3: 3ch (1st tr), 1tr into same place as 3ch, 1tr into next st, *2tr into next st, 1tr into foll st.
Rep from * to end, ss into top of 3ch.
Round 4: 3ch (1st tr), 1tr into next st, 2tr into next st, *1tr into each of next 2sts, 2tr into next st.
Rep from * to end, ss into top of 3ch. (60sts).
Round 5: 3ch (1st tr), 1tr into each of next 2sts, 2tr into next st, *1tr into each of next 3sts, 2tr into next st.
Rep from * to end, ss into top of 3ch.
Round 6: 1ch (1st dc), 1dc into each foll st to end, inc 5dc evenly over round. Ss into 1st dc. (80sts).

◆

SIDE

Round 7: 2ch (1st htr), 1htr into each foll st to end, ss into top of 2ch.
Round 8: (RS) 6ch (1st htr + 4ch), miss next 3sts, *1htr into next st, 4ch, miss next 3sts.
Rep from * to end, ss into 2nd of 6ch. (20sps).
Round 9: 6ch (1st htr + 4ch), *1htr into next htr, working into st slightly left of top of stem, 4ch.
Rep from * to end, ss into 2nd of 6ch.
Rounds 10–13: 7ch (1st htr + 5ch), *1htr into next htr, 5ch.
Rep from * to end, ss into 2nd of 7ch.
Round 14: 8ch (1st htr + 6ch), *1htr into next htr, 6ch. Rep from * to end, ss into 2nd of 8ch.
Round 15: 9ch (1st htr + 7ch), *1htr into next htr, 7ch. Rep from * to end, ss into 2nd of 9ch. Turn.
Round 16: (WS) 5ch. Into same place as 5ch, work (1tr, 2ch) twice and (1tr, 1ch) once. Work 1dc into next 7ch sp, 1ch. *Into next htr (top right), work (1tr, 2ch) 3 times and (1tr, 1ch) once, 1dc into next 7ch sp, 1ch.
Rep from * to end, ss into 3rd of 5ch.
Break yarn and fasten off.

◆

HANDLE

Either use one of the braids described on pages 121-2, or make a twisted cord using 4 strands of crochet cotton and 2 strands of DK yarn – each 1m (1yd) in length (see Techniques).
To complete the basket, apply fabric stiffener. During drying process, adjust slant of htr sts as required and level outer edging of Rnd 16. Place over upturned jar to dry.
Thread handle through two 7ch sps on basket. Knot or loop and stitch ends neatly in place. Coat handle with fabric stiffener, place jar or similar inside basket to prop up handle, and shape handle during drying process.
Cut ribbon in half. Tie two small bows around handle base, above basket rim.

FLORAL CARD

✳ ✳

 Create a nostalgic, feminine greetings card with this pretty embroidery on a padded background. The crochet edging is worked in the same shades of embroidery silk as the central flowers.

◆

MATERIALS

Handkerchief lawn (or any suitable fabric)
16 × 20cm (6¼ × 8in)
Same colour felt 12 × 16cm (4¾ × 6¼in)
6-stranded embroidery silks for leaves, flowers and edging
Embroidery needle
2 pieces foldable card 28 × 18cm (11 × 7in)
and 12 × 16cm (4¾ × 6¼in)
All-purpose adhesive
Felt oddments for flower centres

Hook 1.25

◆

MEASUREMENTS

14 × 18cm (5½ × 7in)

◆

METHOD

1 With 2 strands of silk, smoothly and evenly embroider leaf design centrally on to fabric (see below). Press.
2 Fold larger card down centre to measure 14cm (5½in) wide × 18cm (7in) long.
3 Apply 1cm-wide (½in) strip of glue all around edge of smaller card and affix felt, flattening out from centre. Do not trim.
4 Trim embroidered fabric to approx 1.5cm (¾in) larger all round than smaller card. (Keep embroidery central.)

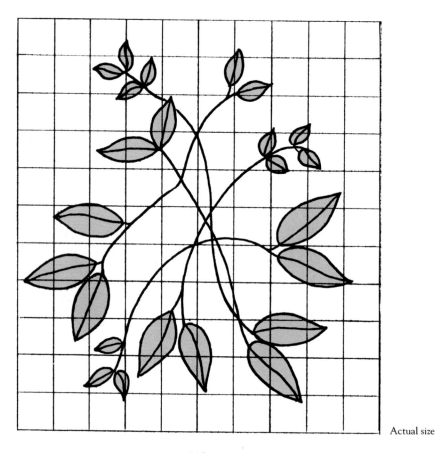

Guide for embroidering leaf and stem tracery onto fabric

Actual size

5 Place felt side of card onto back of embroidery. Keeping fabric fairly taut, turn edges under and glue to back of card, applying extra glue at corners as necessary.

6 Glue centrally onto front of folded card.

7 With 2 strands of silk (or fine crochet cotton oddments), make 2 crocheted flowers following the pattern, and 2 or 3 more flowers with fewer petals.

BASIC FLOWER

Make 7ch. Join with ss into circle.

*Make 8ch, 1tr into 4th ch from hook, 1tr into each of next 3ch, 1htr into next ch, 1dc into circle.

Rep from * until 11 petals. Fasten off.

Arrange flowers on embroidered leaves. Glue backs around centre hole and stick down. Add small circles of felt for flower centres.

EDGING

Make 285ch using 2 strands of embroidery silk. Check ch for (ample) fit around folded fabric edge and adjust sts as necessary.

Row 1: 1htr into 3rd ch from hook, 1htr into each foll ch to end, turn.

Row 2: 3ch (1st tr), 1tr into next st, 3ch, 1htr around stem of last tr made, miss next st, *1tr into each of next 2sts, 3ch, 1htr around stem of last tr made, miss next st.

Rep from * until end of ch is reached.

Break yarn and fasten off.

Glue base ch and 1st row to fabric edge so that frill sits neatly on card edge, making a tiny pinch for corners. Glue frill at corners. Cut edging to correct length and neatly glue down end.

PENNY-FARTHING CARD

❋ ❋

A really Victorian effect is produced with this charming, penny-farthing card. Work the edging in the same way as for the Floral Card.

MATERIALS

Handkerchief lawn (or any suitable fabric)
16 × 20cm (6¼ × 8in)
Same colour felt 12 × 16cm (4¾ × 6¼in)
6-stranded embroidery silks for letters,
bicycle, road and edging
Embroidery needle
2 pieces foldable card 28 × 18cm (11 × 7in)
and 12 × 16cm (4¾ × 6¼in)
All-purpose adhesive
Hook 1.25

MEASUREMENTS

14 × 18cm (5½ × 7in)

METHOD

1 With 2 strands of silk, embroider design, but only mark wheel positions (see p115). Follow Steps 2–6 as for floral card.

7 Crochet a large and small wheel, following instructions.
Press.

LARGE WHEEL

Make 5ch using 2 strands of embroidery silk. Join with ss into circle.

Round 1: 1ch, 10dc into circle, ss into 1st dc.

Round 2: (24ch, 1dc into next dc) 9 times, 24 ch, 1dc into base of 1st 24ch.

Break yarn and fasten off.

Round 3: With RS facing, rejoin to top of any 24ch sp, make 1ch (1st dc), 4dc into same sp, 4ch, *5dc into next sp, 4ch.

Rep from * to end, ss into 1st dc.

Round 4: Into each sp (over 5dc or 4ch), work 5dc. End with ss into 1st dc.

Round 5: 1ch (1st dc), 1dc into each of next 3dc, miss next dc, *1dc into each of next 4dc, miss next dc.

Rep from * to end, ss into 1st dc.

SMALL WHEEL

Make 4ch using 1 strand of embroidery silk. Join with ss into circle.

Round 1: (10ch, 1dc into circle) 6 times. Break yarn and fasten off.

Round 2: With RS facing, rejoin to any 10ch sp, 1ch (1st dc), 2dc into same sp, 3ch, *3dc into next sp, 3ch.

Rep from * to end, ss into 1st dc.

Round 3: Into each sp (over 3dc or 3ch), work 3dc. End with ss into 1st dc.

Round 4: 1ch (1st dc), 1dc into each foll st to end, ss into 1st dc.

Glue centres and rims of wheels and fix into position. Make edging and complete as for floral card.

•

VARIATIONS

1 In place of embroidery, paint on the background using a fabric pen.

2 Using the oval on top of a tissue box as a template, draw an oval centrally onto fabric. Cover drawn line with an edging, and fill oval with miniature crocheted flowers. Complete with a small bow.

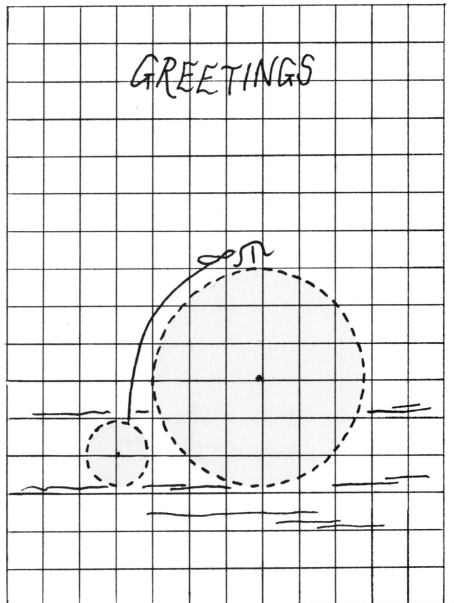

Actual size

Guide for embroidering letters, road marking and bicycle frame onto fabric.
Mark wheel positions, but do not embroider

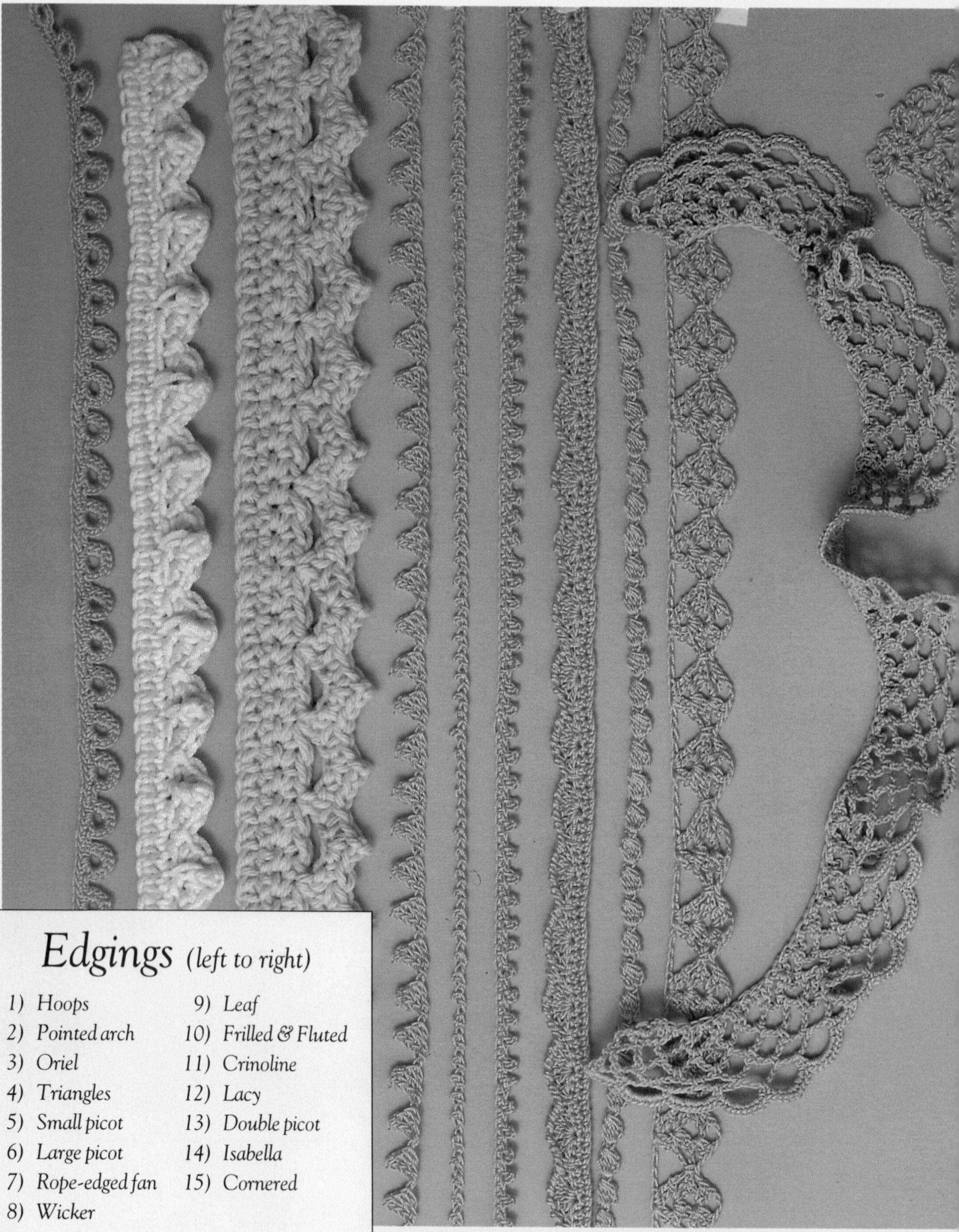

Edgings (left to right)

1) Hoops
2) Pointed arch
3) Oriel
4) Triangles
5) Small picot
6) Large picot
7) Rope-edged fan
8) Wicker
9) Leaf
10) Frilled & Fluted
11) Crinoline
12) Lacy
13) Double picot
14) Isabella
15) Cornered

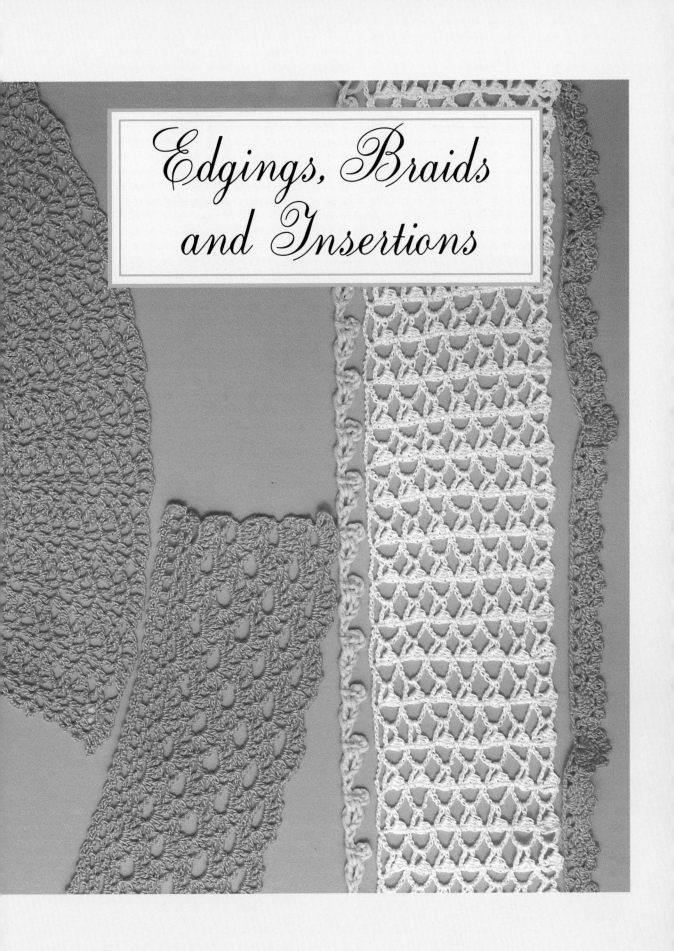

Edgings, Braids and Insertions

Adding a trimming makes all the difference to household items, gifts or clothes, both old and new. Think of an old armchair, for example, given a new lease of life by the addition of an elegant braid around its base, or perhaps bedroom curtains and lampshades tied in with the colour scheme of the room by the clever use of specially made trimmings. There are so many effects you can achieve, simply and quickly, with the thoughtful use of edgings and braids. Insertions can be used either to lengthen or simply decorate. For example, a plain blouse can be transformed into something charming and original with a crochet insertion, either by cutting the fabric and attaching the insertion to both cut edges, or simply by placing the crochet over the fabric and stitching in position.

Braids and insertions can be used in another way, too. Strips can be sewn edge to edge to create attractive fabrics to be used in their own right, for example, for covering cushions or stools. The possibilities are endless, so try some of the effects explained in this chapter, then apply them whenever you like. They may ❧ transform your crochet – and your home!

EDGINGS

◆

HOOPS

Make 6ch. Work 1dc into 6th ch from hook, *9ch, 1dc into 6th ch from hook.
Rep from * to required length.
Work back along straight edge with loops below as follows:
Row 1: 2dc into 1st loop, *1dc into each of next 3ch between loops, 2dc into next loop.
Rep from * to end.
Row 2: With loops above, cont by working another 9dc into 1st loop, *1ss into each of next 3 single base ch opp 3dc grp of last row, 9dc into next loop.
Rep from * to end, ss into 1st st of last row.

◆

POINTED ARCH AND PENDANT

Make a ch divisible by 4 plus 1 to required length.
Row 1: 1dc into 2nd ch from hook, dc to end, turn.
Row 2: (RS) 1ch (1st st), 1dc into each foll dc but instead of working in the usual way, insert hook under and work into each single horizontal st (facing) below top ch of dcs.
(Sts = even no.) Turn.
Row 3: 3ch, miss 1st and next st, 1ss

into each of next 3sts, *3ch, miss next st, 1ss into each of next 3sts.
Rep from * ending with 2ss, turn.
Row 4: 1ch (1st st), miss next ss. *Into next 3ch loop work 2dc, 1dtr (over and in front of loop) into missed st of Row 3. Ease same loop towards left of dtr stem, work 2dc into this loop, 1ss (over ss) into same dc as 2nd of 3ss of Row 3, pull stem and top of dtr forward.
Rep from * but end row with 1dc into edge st.

◆

ORIEL

Make a ch divisible by 3 plus 2 to required length.
Row 1: 1dc into 2nd ch from hook, dc to end, turn.
Rows 2 and 3: 1ch (1st st), dc to end, turn.
Row 4: 5ch, miss 1st and next 2sts, 1ss into next st, *5ch, miss next 2sts, 1ss into next st.
Rep from * to end, turn.
Row 5: 2ch, miss 1st ch st of loop, *1dc into each of next 2 ch sts, 2ch, 1dc into same st as last dc made, 1dc into 4th ch st, (miss 5th ch st, ss and 1st ch st of next loop).
Rep from * working final loop as before but end with 1dc into edge st.

TRIANGLES

*Make 5ch, 1dc into 2nd ch from hook, 1htr into 3rd, 1tr into 4th, 1dtr into 5th ch from hook.
Rep from * to required length.

◆

SMALL PICOT

*Make 3ch, 1dc into 3rd ch from hook.
Rep from * to required length.

◆

LARGE PICOT

(See below)
Make an odd number of ch sts to required length.

A simple picot. Make 3ch. Inserting hook through top and side of last dc made, make 1ss

Work 1dc into 2nd ch from hook, *3ch, insert hook through top loop and left vertical loop of last dc made and make 1ss, 1dc into each of next 2ch.

Rep from * ending with 1dc instead of 2dc.

◆

ROPE-EDGED FAN

Make a ch divisible by 6 plus 2 to required length.

Row 1: 1dc into 2nd ch from hook, dc to end, turn.

Row 2: 1ch (1st st), dc to end, turn.

Row 3:(RS) 1ch (1st st), *miss next 2sts, 6tr into next st, miss next 2sts, 1ss into same dc (in Row 1) as next st (miss dc above).

Rep from * to end working last ss into final st of Row 2. Do not turn.

Row 4: 1ch. Work reverse dc back along trs of Row 3, missing each ss, as follows:

With RS still facing, twist this end of work so as to insert hook (from front) downwards into (normal position) last tr made, yrh, draw yarn through, and complete 1dc as normal.

Rep into each tr until end, 1ss into 1st st of last row.

◆

WICKER

Make 4ch.

4tr bobble into 4th ch from hook (=4tr into one st omitting the 3rd stage of each tr, so that the loops increase on the hook, ie yrh, insert hook into st, yrh, draw loop through, yrh, draw loop through 2 of the loops on hook and omit the foll 3rd stage of the tr. Rep into the same st (4th ch), leaving 3 loops on hook, rep into the same st, leaving 4 loops on hook, rep into the same st, yrh, draw yarn through all 5 loops on hook), *5ch, 4tr bobble into 4th ch from hook.

Rep from * to required length. (Back of work is RS.)

◆

LEAF

Make a ch divisible by 6 minus 2 to required length.

Row 1: (1tr,2ch,2tr) into 4th ch from hook, *5ch, miss next 5 base ch, (2tr,2ch,2tr) into next ch.

Rep from * to end, turn.

Row 2: 3ch, (1tr,2ch,2tr) into 1st 2ch sp, *3ch, (2tr,2ch,2tr) into next 2ch sp.

Rep from * to end, turn.

Row 3: 3ch, (1tr,3ch,2tr) into 1st 2ch sp, *1ch, 1dc under 5ch and 3ch of prev 2 rows, 1ch, (2tr,3ch,2tr) into next 2ch sp.

Rep from * to end, ss into end tr.

◆

FRILLED AND FLUTED

Make a fairly tight ch divisible by 4 minus 2 to required length.

Row 1: 1dc into 6th ch from hook, *5ch, miss next 3 base ch, 1dc into next ch.

Rep from * to end, turn.

Row 2: 5ch, 1dc into 1st 5ch sp, *5ch, 1dc into next 5ch sp.

Rep from * to end (including last sp), turn.

Rep last row 12 times more, or as required.

Final row: (RS) 10dc into each 5ch sp. Break yarn and fasten off.

For gathered heading: with RS facing, work along base ch edge, join yarn, make 1ch, and make 1dc into each 3ch sp with 1tr into each dc stem.

If desired, a length of narrow ribbon can be threaded through top row of spaces.

◆

CRINOLINE

Make 5ch, 1ss into 5th ch from hook, *12ch, 1ss into 5th ch from hook.

Rep from * to required length.

Row 1: 4ch. Working along ss side of base ch: into 1st loop, over ss, work (1tr,1ch,1tr), 6ch, *(keep base ch untwisted), 1tr into next loop, (1ch,1tr) twice into same loop, 6ch.

Rep from * to last loop, (1tr,1ch) twice into loop, make another 3ch, 1ss into same loop.

Row 2: Working back along opp side of loops:

4ch, (1tr,1ch) 4 times into 1st loop, *1dc around centre of next 7ch, 1ch, (1tr,1ch) 4 times into next loop.

Rep from * to end.

Work 1 extra tr into last loop, turn.

Row 3: Ss to and into 2nd sp between trs, 5ch, 1tr into same sp, (2ch,1tr) twice into each of next 2sps, *(miss next 2 sps). Over next centre 3sps, (1tr,2ch,1tr) into 1st sp, (2ch,1tr) twice into each of foll 2sps.

Rep from * to end disregarding final sp, turn.

Rep last row to required depth.

◆

LACY

Make a ch divisible by 8 plus 4 to required length.

Row 1: 1tr into 6th ch from hook, *1ch, miss next ch, 1tr into next ch.

Rep from * to end.

Row 2: Work along base ch side, 4ch, 1dc into 1st sp, *3ch, 1dc into next sp.

Rep from * to end.

Row 3: Working along straight edge, rep last row, working (again) into 1st sp but not last loop, turn.

Cont on same side.

Row 4: 2dc into 1st 3ch sp, *5ch, miss next 3ch, 1dc into next 3ch sp.

Rep from * to end, turn.

Row 5: 1dc into 1st 5ch sp, 5ch. Into same sp, work (2tr,2ch) twice and 1tr. *2ch, 1dc into next 5ch sp, 2ch. Into next sp, work a scallop – (1tr,2ch,1tr) 3 times.

Rep from * to end, turn.

Row 6: 1dc into 1st sp, 6ch, miss next (centre) sp of scallop, 1dc into next sp, *5ch, miss next 2sps in-between, 1dc into 1st sp of next scallop, 6ch, 1dc into 3rd sp of same scallop.

Rep from * to end, turn.

Row 7: 1dc into 1st sp, 5ch, 1dc into both 1st (6ch sp and centre 2ch sp of prev row) tog, 2ch, *(1tr,2ch,1tr) 3 times into next 5ch sp, 2ch, 1dc into both next (6ch sp and centre 2ch sp of prev row) tog, 2ch.

Rep from * to end, 1tr into end dc, turn.

Row 8: 1dc into 1st sp, 5ch, *1dc into 1st sp of next 3-sp scallop, 6ch, miss centre sp of scallop, 1dc into next sp, 5ch, miss 2 sps in-between.

Braids

1) Epaulette
2) Elizabeth
3) Sailor's Scroll
4) Slip-stitch cord
5) Two-piece
6) Wheels
7) Firestone
8) Cannich loops
   (two examples)
9) Abigail
10) Two colours

Rep from * to end, 1dc into end dc, turn.

Row 9: 1dc into 1st sp, 5ch. Into same sp, work (2tr,2ch) twice and 1tr. *2ch, 1dc into both next (6ch sp and centre 2ch sp of prev row) tog, 2ch, (1tr,2ch,1tr) 3 times into next 5ch sp.

Rep from * to end, turn.

Rep Rows 6–9 to required depth.

◆

DOUBLE PICOT

*Make 4ch, 1tr into 3rd ch from hook, 4ch, 1dc into last loop made.

Rep from * to required length.

ISABELLA

Make 41ch (or any no divisible by 5 plus 1 to required depth).

Row 1: 1dc into 11th ch from hook, *7ch, miss next 4 base ch, 1dc into next ch.

Rep from * to end, turn.

Row 2: (RS) 7ch, 2dtr into 1st loop.

(Insert hook from front into sp between last 2dtr made), work (1dc, 1htr,1tr) around last dtr stem, *2dtr into next loop, (1dc,1htr,1tr) around last dtr stem.

Rep from * to last loop, (1dtr,1ttr) into loop, (1dc,1htr,1tr) around ttr stem.

Ease dtrs to loop centres of prev row. Turn.

Row 3: Miss ttr, 1dtr into 1st dtr, 6ch, 1dc into sp (diamond-shaped) between 1st dtr and foll tr, *7ch, miss next dtr pair, 1dc into same-shaped sp, just before foll tr.

Rep from * to last loop, 7ch, 1dc into 7ch sp (over 7th of 7ch), turn.

Rep last 2 rows to required length.

This edging can be left as it is, or gathered along looped edge.

◆

CORNERED

Make 4ch, *1dc into 4th ch from hook (corner loop made), 9ch, (1tr into 4th ch from hook, 9ch) required no of times to position for next corner loop.

Rep from * to fit rem sides, omitting 4ch sts at end, ss (untwisted) into 1st st.

Row 1: 1ss into 1st loop, 3ch(tr), 8tr into same loop, (1tr,2ch,1tr) into 3rd of next 5ch, *7tr into next loop – ease sts tog towards loop centre, (1tr,2ch,1tr) into 3rd of next 5ch.

Rep from * to end, but working 9tr into each corner loop.

Row 2: Into each of 1st, 3rd, 5th, 7th and 9th tr of next 9tr group, work (1ss,4ch,1tr into 4th ch from hook = rose), miss next (1tr,2ch,1tr).

*Into each of 1st, 3rd, 5th and 7th tr of next 7tr group, work a rose, miss next (1tr,2ch,1tr).

Rep from * to end, but working an extra rose at each corner. Ss into 1st st.

BRAIDS

◆

EPAULETTE

Make a ch divisible by 3 minus 1 to required length.

Row 1: 1dc into 2nd ch from hook, dc to end, turn.

Row 2: (RS) 2ch (1st st), 1htr into next st, *(loosen loop on hook). Around stem of last htr made, work 1st stage of 1tr as follows:

Yrh, insert hook (from the front) under stem, yrh, bring hooked loop forward (3 loops on hook). Work 2 more 1st stages around same stem, yrh, draw through all 7 loops on hook. Miss next free dc, 1htr into each of next 2sts.

Rep from * ending row with only 1htr, turn.

Row 3: 2ch (1st st), dc evenly to end.

ELIZABETH

Make 6ch.

Row 1: Work 2tr into 3rd ch from hook, miss 2ch, 1dc into end ch, turn.

Row 2: 3ch, 2tr into 3rd ch from hook, miss next 2tr worked in last row, 1dc into top of end 2ch, turn.

Rep Row 2 to required length.

◆

SAILOR'S SCROLL

Make ch to required length.

Keeping final loop of each st fairly tight, work 1dtr into 5th ch from hook, dtr to end. Do not turn. Work 4dc around end dtr stem. Twisting and turning work as necessary, with same side still facing, work 1dc around and enclosing base ch between last 2dtr made.

Turn work clockwise and work 4dc around next (2nd) dtr stem.

Turn to reverse side and work 1dc (enclosing top of dtrs) between 2nd and 3rd dtr.

Turn to front again, 4dc around next (3rd) dtr stem, 1dc around base ch between 3rd and 4th dtrs.

Cont to end, working the 4dc from the front around every dtr, and 1dc alternately along sides. (1dc between every two dtr along an edge.)

SLIP-STITCH CORD

Make ch to required length.

Work 1ss into 2nd and each foll single horizontal st behind each ch.

TWO-PIECE

(Use yarn in two colours of equal thickness.) With 1st colour, *make 3ch, 1dc into 3rd ch from hook.
Rep from * to required length. Break off 1st colour.
Do not turn – work Row 1 back along straighter edge.
Row 1: (RS) Join 2nd colour with 2ch, 1dc into st above 1st picot, work a 2nd dc into part of ch st showing between 1st 2 picots, 1dc into st above 2nd picot.
Cont similarly to end (with 1dc between picots and 1dc above each picot). Work 1dc after final picot.
Make another piece exactly the same.
Line up opposite picots and sew the 2 pieces together on WS along straight edges.

WHEELS

Make 5ch. Join with ss into circle.
Row 1: 2ch, work 9htr into circle, ss into top of 2ch.
Row 2: 7ch, (1dtr into next htr, 3ch) 9 times, ss into 4th of 7ch.
Row 3: 1ch, 1dc into same place as 1ch, 3dc into next sp, *2dc into next dtr, 3dc into next sp.
Rep from * to end, ss into 1ch.
Row 4: 1ss into each foll st to end.
Make 14ch. Work 1ss into 5th ch from hook, to make a circle. Keeping the 9 linking ch behind work, rep from Row 1 to required length.

FIRESTONE

Make ch to required length.
(RS facing) Picking up top strand only for all sts, work 1dc into 2nd ch from hook, dc to end. Break yarn and fasten off. Rejoining at slip-knot, make 2ch for 1st st, dc back along opp side of ch picking up single strands as before. Break yarn, fasten off and sew in ends.
The braid can be used as it is, or decorated in a variety of ways. Some suggestions:
1 Weave narrow ribbon through central eyelets.
2 Crochet a chain along centre; or make a separate chain and sew down with another colour.

CANNICH LOOPS

*Make 3ch, 1tr into 3rd ch from hook. Rep from * to required length.
Round 1: 3ch, 1dc around tr stem into 1st loop, *3ch, 1dc into next loop.
Rep from * to end.
Work around end with (3ch, 1dc into same loop) twice.
Cont back along unworked side with the same patt, (3ch, 1dc into next loop) to end.
Work another 3ch, 1dc into same end loop, ss into 1st loop of round.

ABIGAIL

Make 5ch.
Row 1: 1htr into 3rd ch from hook, 1htr into each of next 2ch, turn.

Row 2: 2ch (1st htr), 1htr between 1st 2htr, 1htr between 2nd and 3rd htr, 1htr between 3rd and 4th htr, turn.
Rep last row until required length. Do not turn after final row.
Over stem of end htr of each row, work along edge: 1ss over 1st htr stem, *2dc over next htr stem, 1ss over next htr stem.
Rep from * to end of braid.
With same side facing, similarly complete 2nd edge, with 2dc opp 2dc, 1ss opp 1ss.

TWO COLOURS

With col A, make no of ch divisible by 4 to required length.
Row 1: (RS) 1tr into 4th ch from hook, *2ch, miss next 2ch, 1tr into each of next 2ch.
Rep from * to end. Break yarn and fasten off.
Row 2: (RS facing) Join col B between 1st 2tr. Work along edge: 1ch, *5dc into next 2ch sp, 1ss between next 2tr.
Rep from * to end. Break yarn and fasten off. Work similarly along 2nd edge.
Row 3: (RS facing) Join col A between 1st 2tr of Row 1, 3ch (tr), tr3tog (including 1st tr) in same place. *Over next 5dc, miss 1st dc, 1dc into each of next 3dc, miss next dc, tr3tog inserting hook between next 2tr of Row 1.
Rep from * to end.
Work similarly along 2nd edge.

INSERTIONS

FILET

Make 18ch.
Row 1: 1tr into 4th ch from hook, 1tr into each of next 5ch, 2ch, miss

next 2ch, 1tr into each of next 7ch, turn.
Row 2: (First 3ch counts as 1st tr in this and foll rows.) 3ch, 1tr into each

of next 3sts, 2ch, miss next 2sts, 1tr into next st, 2tr into next 2ch sp, 1tr into next st, 2ch, miss next 2sts, 1tr into each of next 4sts, turn.

Row 3: 3ch, 1tr into each of next 3sts, 2ch, miss next 2ch, 1tr into next st, 2ch, miss next 2sts, 1tr into next st, 2ch, miss next 2ch, 1tr into each of next 4sts, turn.

Row 4: 3ch, 1tr into each of next 3sts, 2ch, miss next 2ch, 1tr into next st, 2tr into next 2ch sp, 1tr into next st, 2ch, miss next 2ch, 1tr into each of next 4sts, turn.

Row 5: 3ch, 1tr into each of next 3sts, 2tr into next 2ch sp, 1tr into next st, 2ch, miss next 2sts, 1tr into next st, 2tr into next 2ch sp, 1tr into each of next 4sts, turn.

Rep Rows 2-5 until required length is reached.

LONG CHECKERS

Make 18ch.

Row 1: 1dtr into 5th ch from hook, 1dtr into next ch, (3ch, miss next 3ch, 1dtr into each of next 3ch) twice, turn.

Row 2: 6ch, miss 1st 3dtr block, 1dtr into each of next 3ch, 3ch, miss next 3dtr, 1dtr into each of next 3ch, 2ch, miss next 2dtr, 1dtr into end st, turn.

Row 3: 4ch (dtr), 1dtr into each of next 2ch, (3ch, miss next 3dtr, 1dtr into each of next 3ch) twice, turn.

Rep last 2 rows to required length.

BUTTONS

*Make 3ch, 1tr into 3rd ch from hook.

Rep from * to required length with even no of trs.

Round 1: 3ch, 1dc around tr stem into 1st loop, *3ch, 1dc into next loop.

Rep from * to end. Work (3ch,1dc into same end loop) twice more. Mark last loop made.

Rep from * along unworked side to end, working only 1 extra loop into end loop, instead of 2. This is last loop of 2nd side. Do not turn.

Round 2: 2dc into 1st 3ch loop of Rnd 1. Work (7tr into next loop, 1dc into foll loop) to marked loop. Make another dc into last loop, 2ch, 2dc into marked loop.

Work (7tr into next loop, 1dc into foll loop) to end of 2nd side, making another dc into last loop. 2ch, 1ss into 1st dc of round.

Round 3: 7ch, (1dc,2ch,1dc) into 4th of next 7tr, *6ch, (1dc,2ch,1dc) into 4th of next 7tr.

Rep from * to end of 1st side, 7ch, 3dc into 2ch sp, 7ch, (1dc,2ch,1dc) into 4th of next 7tr.

Rep from * to end of 2nd side, 7ch, 3dc into 2ch sp.

Round 4: 7ch, 1htr into 6th ch st of next 7ch, 2ch, 1htr into next ch st, 2ch, *1htr into 1st ch st of next 6ch, 2ch, 1htr into next ch st, 2ch, 1htr into 5th ch st of same 6ch, 2ch, 1htr into next ch st, 2ch.

Rep from * to end of 6ch loops, 1st side.

Work 1htr into 1st ch st of next 7ch, 2ch, 1htr into next ch st, 7ch, 1dc into each of next 3dc, 7ch. Starting with 6th of next 7ch, cont same patt of htrs and chs to end. Work into 1st and 2nd ch sts of last 7ch, make 7ch, 1dc into each of next 2dc, 1ss into next dc.

SPIDER FLOWER

Make 28ch.

Row 1: 1tr into 7th ch from hook, 1tr into each of next 18ch, 2ch, miss 2ch, 1tr into last ch, turn.

Row 2: 5ch, miss 1st tr and next 2ch, 1tr into each of next 7tr, 4ch, miss next 2tr, 1dtr into next tr, 4ch, miss next 2tr, 1tr into each of next 7tr, 2ch, miss 2ch, 1tr into next ch, turn.

Row 3: 5ch, miss 1st tr and next 2ch, 1tr into each of next 5tr, 4ch, 1dc into 4th of next 4ch, 1dc into dtr, 1dc into 1st of next 4ch, 4ch, miss next 2tr, 1tr into each of next 5tr, 2ch, miss 2ch, 1tr into next ch, turn.

Row 4: 5ch, miss 1st tr and next 2ch, 1tr into each of next 3tr, 6ch, 1dc into each of 3dc, 6ch, miss next 2tr, 1tr into each of next 3tr, 2ch, miss 2ch, 1tr into next ch, turn.

Row 5: 5ch, miss 1st tr and next 2ch, 1tr into each of next 3tr, 2tr

into 6ch sp, 5ch, 1dc into each of 3dc, 5ch, 2tr into next 6ch sp, 1tr into each of next 3tr, 2ch, miss 2ch, 1tr into next ch, turn.

Row 6: 5ch, miss 1st tr and next 2ch, 1tr into each of next 5tr, 2tr into 5ch sp, 2ch, 1dtr into centre dc, 2ch, 2tr into next 5ch sp, 1tr into each of next 5tr, 2ch, miss 2ch, 1tr into next ch, turn.

Row 7: 5ch, miss 1st tr and next 2ch, 1tr into each of next 7tr, 2tr into next 2ch sp, 1tr into dtr, 2tr into next 2ch sp, 1tr into each of next 7tr, 2ch, miss 2ch, 1tr into next ch, turn.

Rep Rows 2–7 to required length.

JACOB'S LADDER

Make 12ch.

Row 1: 1tr into 4th ch from hook, 1tr into next ch, 4ch, miss 4ch, 1tr into each of next 3ch, turn.

Row 2: 3ch (tr), 1tr into each of next 2tr, 4ch, miss 4ch, 1tr into each of next 3tr, turn.

Rep last row to required length.

DAISY RINGS

Make 4ch, 1dtr into 4th ch from hook, *6ch, 1dtr into 4th ch from hook.

Rep from * to required length. Do not turn.

Round 1: (1st side) Around dtr, into 1st loop, work petals as follows: 1dc and (3ch,1dc) 5 times into same loop, *1ch to next loop, 1dc and (3ch, 1dc) 5 times into loop.

Rep from * to end.

Make 3ch. Do not turn.

(2nd side) Into same end loop, work 1dc and (3ch,1dc) 5 times. With petals opposite petals, rep the 1ch and petals patt to end.

Make 3ch, 1ss into 1st dc. Do not turn.

Round 2: (1st side) 9ch, 1tr into space of 3rd of 1st 5 petals, *5ch, 1tr into space of 3rd of next 5 petals.

Rep from * to end, 9ch, miss 4th and 5th petals, 1ss into next petal.

Work 2nd side to match 1st side.

Insertions

1) Filet
2) Long Checkers
3) Buttons
4) Spider Flower
5) Jacob's Ladder
6) Daisy Rings
7) Wheatsheaf
8) Six-Petal Flower
9) Diamond Zig Zag
10) Picot Motif

WHEATSHEAF

Make 12ch.

Row 1: 1tr into 4th ch from hook, 7ch, miss 6 base ch, 1tr into each of next 2ch, turn.

Row 2: 3ch (1st tr), 1tr into next tr, 6ch, miss 7ch, 1tr into each of next 2tr, turn.

Row 3: 3ch (1st tr), 1tr into next tr, 3ch, 1dc into sp to enclose 6ch and 7ch of prev 2 rows, 3ch, 1tr into each of next 2tr, turn.

Row 4: 3ch (1st tr), 1tr into next tr, 7ch, 1tr into each of next 2tr, turn.

Rep Rows 2–4 to required length, working final row of insertion as Row 4 but with 6ch instead of 7ch. Do not turn after final row.

Work 1st side as follows: 1ch, insert hook into sp between last 2tr of final row, and work 2dc to enclose outer tr stem, *8ch, miss next 2sps along edge, 2dc into next sp.

Rep from * to end. Make 11ch.

Complete 2nd side to match 1st side, ending with 10ch and 1ss into 1st st.

SIX-PETAL FLOWER

This insertion can be made of one or more strips of flowers, sewn together, to any depth required.

Make 12ch. Join with ss into circle.

Round 1: 1ch, 24dc into circle, ss into 1st dc.

Round 2: 9ch, (miss next dc, 1ss into each of next 3dc, 9ch) 5 times, miss next dc, 1ss into each of next 2dc.

Round 3: *1ss into 1st st of next 9ch, 1dc into each of next 3ch sts, 3dc into next st at centre of ch loop, 1dc into each of next 3ch sts, 1ss into next st. Rep from * to end, ss into 1st st of round. Leave 20cm (8in) end. Break yarn and fasten off. Make the no required, and join together.

To make a ch edging: with RS facing, join yarn to 1st petal tip, *7ch, 1dtr into sp between next 2 petals, 7ch, 1dc into next petal tip. Rep from * to end.

Work similarly along rem edge.

The pattern produced when six-petal flower motifs are sewn together

DIAMOND ZIG-ZAG

Make 22ch, fairly loosely.

Row 1: 1dc into 6th ch from hook, *3ch, miss next base ch, 1dc into next ch.

Rep from * to end, turn.

Row 2: 3ch, 1dc into 1st loop, 3ch, 1dc into next loop, *3tr into next dc, 1dc into next loop, (3ch, 1dc) into each of next 2 loops.

Rep from * once more, 3ch, 1dc into last loop, turn.

Row 3: 3ch, 1dc into 1st loop, *(3ch,1dc) into each of next 2 loops, 3tr into next dc, 1dc into 2nd of next 3tr.

Rep from * once more, (3ch,1dc) into each of next 2 loops, turn.

Row 4: 3ch, 1dc into 1st loop, 3ch, 1dc into next loop, 3ch, *1dc into 2nd of next 3tr, 3tr into next dc, (1dc,3ch) into each of next 2 loops.

Rep from * once more, 1dc into last loop, turn.

Row 5: 3ch, 1dc into 1st loop, 3ch, 1dc into next loop, *3tr into next dc, 1dc into 2nd of next 3tr, (3ch,1dc) into each of next 2 loops.

Rep from * once more, 3ch, 1dc into last loop, turn.

Rep Rows 3–5 to required length.

PICOT MOTIF

(Sewn directly onto fabric. Work 2 or 3 rounds.)

Make 5ch. Join with ss into circle.

Round 1: 3ch (1st tr), (4ch, 1dc into 3rd ch from hook = picot, 1ch, 1tr into circle) 5 times, picot, 1ch, ss into 1st tr. (6 picots).

Note the single ch st at each side of picots.

Round 2: Ss into ch st before 1st picot, 3ch (1st tr), (picot, 1ch, 1tr into next ch st of prev round) 11 times to end.

Work 1 picot, 1ch, ss into 1st tr. (12 picots).

Round 3: 3ch (1st tr), picot, 1ch, miss 1st ch st of prev round, 1tr into ch st between 1st picot and foll tr, picot, 1ch, 1tr into ch st between same tr and foll picot, picot, 1ch, (1tr into next tr, picot, 1ch, miss next ch st of prev round, 1tr into ch st between next picot and foll tr, picot, 1ch, 1tr into ch st between same tr and foll picot, picot, 1ch) 5 times, ss into 1st tr. (18 picots).

Yarn Manufacturers/ Suppliers

Coats Patons Crafts
P O Box, McMullen Road, Darlington, Co Durham
DL1 1YQ
Tel: 0325 381010

DMC Creative World Ltd
Pullman Road, Wigston, Leicester, LE18 2DY
Tel: 0533 811040

Jaeger Handknitting Ltd
McMullen Road, Darlington, Co Durham DL1 1YQ
Tel: 0325 380123

Jarol Ltd
White Rose Mills, Cape Street, Canal Road,
Bradford, BD1 4RN
Tel: 0274 392274

Sirdar Ltd
Flanshaw Lane, Alverthorpe, Wakefield,
West Yorkshire WF2 9ND
Tel: 0924 371501

Twilleys of Stamford Ltd
Roman Mill, Stamford, Lincs PE9 1BG
Tel: 0780 52661

◆

AUSTRALIA

Coats Patons Handknittings
89–91 Peters Avenue, Mulgrave, Victoria 3170
Tel: 03 5612288

DMC Needlecraft Pty Ltd
51–66 Carrington Road, Marrickville, NSW 2204
Tel: 02 5593088

Panda Yarns Pty
314–320 Albert Street, Brunswick,
Victoria 3056
Tel: 03 3803888

◆

USA

Coats & Clark Inc
30 Patewood Drive, Suite 351, Greenville,
SC29615
Tel: 803 2340331

The DMC Corporation
Port Kearny, Building 10, South Kearny,
NJ07032
Tel: 201 5890606

Knitting Fever Inc
180 Babylon Turnpike, Roosevelt, NY11575
Tel: 516 5463600

Plymouth Yarn Co Inc
500 Lafayette Street, Bristol, PA19007
Tel: 215 7880459

Rainbow Gallery Inc
7412 Fulton Avenue, North Hollywood,
California 91605
Tel: 818 9824496

Index

Abbreviations, 2
Antimacassar, 33

Baby shawl, 98
Babywear, 92–9
Bag, 23
Balls, 79, 103, 104
Base chain see Stitches
Basin holders, 54
Basket, 111
Bathmat, 82
Bathroom, 80–7
Bedlinen edgings, 72
Bedspread, 70
Bedroom, 68–79
Bell, 102
Blanket, 38
Blocking and pressing, 15
Bobble, 110, 119
Bonnet, 96
Bookmark, 30
Boot, 104
Braids, 121–2
Butterflies and flowers chart, 90

Cake frill, 62
Canopy and frill, 90
Cards, 112–15
Celebration, 102–15
Chain see Stitches
Changing colour, 11
Chest cover see Table-top
Christmas, ball, 103; bell, 102; ribbon, 102
Christmas decorations see Decorations
Christmas tree chart, 14
Christmas tree fairy, 106
Circles, 10–11, 34
Coffee jar cover, 47
Cord, 15, 121
Corners, 33–6, 121
Curtains, 18, 84
Cushions, 38, 76

Decorations, 102–10
Decreasing, 10, 13 see also Multiples
Diamond patterns, 59–60, 126
Doily, 58
Door curtain, 18
Double chain, 9
Double crochet see Stitches
Double treble see Stitches
Dress, baby, 92
Duchesse set, 73

Edgings (trimmings), 117–21
Egg cosy, 48
Embroidered gifts, 40, 112, 114
Equipment, 6

Fairy, 106
Fastening off, 8
Felled seam, 108
Filet crochet, 11–14; bedlinen edgings, 72, 73; door curtain, 18; guest towel edging, 83; insertions, 122; jam pot cover, 50; nursery valance, 90; practice piece for shaping, 13; shelf edging, 50; techniques, 11–13
Floral card, 112
Flowerpot cover, 21
Flowers, 22, 114, 123, 126; in filet, 12, 14, 90
Frame, 35

Galleon chart, 18
Gloves, 26
'Granny' squares, 33
Guest towel edging, 83
Guitar chart, 14

Half treble see Stitches
Hall, 17–27
Heart, 104
Hooks, 6
Hot water bottle cover, 71

Ice cream border, 46
Increasing, 10, 13 see also Multiples
Insertions, 122–6

Jam pot cover, 50
Jug cover, 51

Key bookmark, 30
Kitchen, 44–55

Lacet see Stitches
Lacy doily, 58
Ladies' gloves, 26
Lampshade, 31
Lavender bags, 86
Leaves, 21, 22, 112, 119
Living room, 28–43

Matinée coat, 94
Motifs, bedspread, 70; canopy and frill, 90; key bookmark, 30; napkin ring, 67; picot insertions, 126; snow crystal, 105; sofa throwover, 33; tablecloth, 60
Multiples, 6

Napkin ring, 67
Needlecase, 40
Notes, 6
Nursery, 89–99

Penny-farthing card, 114
Picot, edgings, 118, 121; motif, 126; needlecase, 40

Picture frame, 35
Pillowcase edging, 73
Pineapple design (jug cover), 51–4
Place mat, 42
Plant hanging, 55
Playing cards envelope, 32
'Popcorn' motif, 67, 71
Pressing, 15
Purse, 20

Ribbon, 102
Rose chart, 12
Rug, 49

Sewing, 15
Shamrock design, 21
Shaping, 10, 13
Shawls, 23, 98
Sheet edging, 72
Shelf edging, 50
Slip-knot, 7
Snow crystal, 105
Snowman, 109
Sofa throwover, 33
Spider flower, 58–9, 123
Spirals, 10–11, 55
Stiffening, 109, 111
Stitches, 7–9; chain, 7, 9; double chain, 9; double crochet, 8, 119; double treble, 9; half treble, 8; lacet, 13, 83; slip stitch, 8, 121; treble, 9; triple treble, 9

Table centre, 42
Tablecloth, 60
Table runner, 19
Table-top (chest cover), 74
Tassel, 75
Tea cosy, 63
Teapot chart, 14
Teatime, 56–67
Techniques, 6, 7–15
Tension, 6
Tissue box cover, 87
Toilet roll cover, 82
Towel edging, 83
Tower Bridge chart, 51
Traycloth, 59
Triangles, 46, 118
Trimmings, 15, 117–26
Turning chains, 6, 9
Twisted cord, 15

Valances, 46, 90

Wave pattern, 82
Wheels, 114, 122
'Windows' cushion, 38
Working in rounds, 10–11

Yarns, 6, 127